IMAGES
of England

ARMTHORPE, HATFIELD, STAINFORTH AND THORNE

Children in fancy dress take part in the Hatfield Woodhouse Feast, August 1909. From left to right they are: Bullar Morris, Mildred Fiddler, Mary Morris, Alice White.

IMAGES
of England

ARMTHORPE, HATFIELD, STAINFORTH AND THORNE

Compiled by
Peter Tuffrey

TEMPUS

First published 1999
Copyright © Peter Tuffrey, 1999

Tempus Publishing Limited
The Mill, Brimscombe Port,
Stroud, Gloucestershire, GL5 2QG

ISBN 0 7524 0620 5

Typesetting and origination by
Tempus Publishing Limited
Printed in Great Britain by
Midway Clark Printing, Wiltshire

Hatfield church choir. Included among those pictured are: James Fiddler (church warden) and Frank Meredith Brookes (vicar).

Contents

Acknowledgements

I would like to thank the following people for their help: Norman Barrass, K. Bowling, Alan Dosdson, Ken Elliff, Mildred Fiddler, Mrs Hilton, Hugh Parkin, Mike Taylor, and Tristram Tuffrey.

Introduction

This is a further book in a series of books I have produced to feature several communities within the sprawling Doncaster Metropolitan Borough Council area. Armthorpe, Hatfield, Stainforth and Thorne are to the east of Doncaster town centre, and each section contains fascinating photographs, some of which were taken by Doncaster-based photographer Edgar Leonard Scrivens – who was the subject of a book himself at one time. Among the other pictures are some taken by the relatively unknown picture postcard photographer, Reg Elliff.

A number of the Armthorpe pictures are centred on the main thoroughfare, winding through the village and aptly showing the scene prior to changes brought about by the colliery – Markham Main. In these early pictures we see a leisurely, rural existence with people posing on unmade, empty roads. At this time, people like Plough Inn licensee Hannah Slater were the well respected pillars of the community – owning land and property. The school where the remarkably clean and well dressed children posed has been swept away, along with many other buildings along the thoroughfare. In fact, it is now becoming increasingly difficult to compare the old pictures with the scene today, as so much redevelopment has occurred during the intervening years. I spent several hours myself walking up and down getting my bearings, discovering what had gone and what remained. For a number of the Armthorpe pictures, I am indebted to Geoff Thomas and Alan Dodson, the latter being a well known Armthorpe historian. Alan allowed me to use certain photographs, which I list among my personal favourites. These were taken by the acclaimed photographer Bert Hardy and show scenes at the time of the visit to Armthorpe (during the Second World War) by writer J.B. Priestley, who was researching an article. Perhaps my two favourites from the entire group are on pages 30 and 31. An impromptu tap dance by the daughter of Mr and Mrs Bell is shown on page 30, full of charm and perhaps not without a touch of humour. The interior of a miner's home shown on page 31 provides a unique glimpse into housing conditions at the time. Sadly, Markham Main is no more and many of the changes that will ensue remain to be seen.

Many of the Hatfield pictures are also concentrated on the main street winding through the area. However, in contrast to Armthorpe, many of the old properties depicted still survive today. In fact, it may be argued, that perhaps not too many changes would be noticed at all, if it were not for the traffic thundering through – as it does in spite of the M18, which was supposed to take traffic away from the village!

Hatfield has some splendid buildings, retaining many original features, however, the whole character of the area has altered as it is now a dormitory village, with very few people actually working in the area. It was difficult to decide whether to put the colliery pictures in the Hatfield or Stainforth sections as the colliery is nearer the latter. However, it has always been referred to as Hatfield Colliery and never to my knowledge as the Stainforth Colliery, so the pictures have fallen into the Hatfield section. My only disappointment with Hatfield was that I could not locate any pictures of the brewery owned by William Winder. I can only hope that this book may encourage someone to contact me and say they have some!

I am pleased that in the next section, I was able to find pictures showing old and new Stainforth. Some of the older pictures give an indication of Stainforth's connection with the waterways. The illustration dominating page 70 is very evocative, especially when making a comparison with the relatively desolate scene today. Other pictures of Stainforth show how it grew with the influx of miners to Hatfield Colliery.

Photographs in the Thorne section show the town's association with waterways, brewing and the peat industry. A dramatic 'then and now' comparison of Waterside is shown – this area was once a hive of activity, however not only have a number of the buildings disappeared, so has the river itself! Discovering this at first hand was quite an experience. While I walked round Thorne town centre, familiarizing myself with various buildings and streets, I could not help but remember that I, along with countless others, once crawled through Thorne on the way to the east coast. How the town once coped with all that traffic moving slowly bumper to bumper before the motorway is incredible.

Once more I will end with the hope that you enjoy looking at this book as much as I have enjoyed compiling it.

Peter Tuffrey
April 1999

One

Armthorpe

View of Church Street looking south. At this time Armthorpe, three and a half miles to the north east of Doncaster, was a farming village with one straggling main street. Earl Fitzwilliam DSO was lord of the manor; the trustees of Robert John Bentley of West House, Rotherham and the trustees of W.H. De Rhodes were the chief landowners. During the first decade of the present century, there were over a dozen farmers noted in the village. The chief crops were wheat, and barley. The population in 1901 was 314. By 1911 it was 381. Victoria cottages may be seen in the distance on the left. The scene here is unrecognizable today.

Victoria Cottages on Church Street, looking south. In 1922 Abercrombie and Johnson mentioned: 'Until recently [Armthorpe was] a small rural village. [But] with the advent of the new colliery and the housing developments in connection with the same, its character has entirely changed and is changing. The original straggling village street of a mile in length is bound to develop as an offshoot of the colliery village, which lies at the opposite end nearer Doncaster.'

Farm cottages on Church Street, facing south. The picture was taken slightly in front of the view above.

White House Farm on Church Street, which is one of a very small number of buildings that survive today, to remind us of the thoroughfare's appearance in times past. A former occupant of this property was Mrs Taylor.

Scholey House, formerly owned by George Scholey, was used as a post office during the early years of the present century, being demolished in 1937. During the Edwardian period Miss Esther Park was the sub-postmistress. Letters arrived from Doncaster, and were delivered at 6.50 a.m. Letters were despatched to Doncaster at 7.45 p.m. Interestingly, there was also a wall letter box, near the church – this was cleared at 6.45 a.m. and 7.35 p.m. on week days only.

Two views of Church Street, looking south, featuring Eastleigh Farm and Woodleigh House. The latter property was formerly occupied by Joseph Appleyard. Also to be seen above is the Primitive Methodist chapel, which was built in 1832.

Church Street, looking north, with the Plough Inn on the left. Licensee Hannah Slater, whose name may be seen on the pub's sign, died in 1912. Her obituary noted that her death cast quite a gloom over the village and immediate neighbourhood, for her unassuming disposition had gained her widespread popularity. 'Deceased who was in her 75th year, was a native of Askham, and was the widow of Thomas Slater, who pre-deceased her 26 years ago, and at one time the occupier of Glebe Farm, Armthorpe. Since her husband's death she had conducted the 'house' which has been in the family for a large number of years without intermission…She was also the owner of a considerable amount of property in the village, and was the oldest freehold owner on the award of Armthorpe.'

Church Street, looking north. On the right is the entrance to the Church School.

Armthorpe National School, with children posing outside. Armthorpe Public Elementary School (mixed) was built in 1842 and endowed with 2a 3r 34p (acres, roods and perches). of land allotted at the inclosure in 1754 which at the turn of the century was let for £3. There was also a sum of £2 10s paid out of the Bella Hall Estate, Grimston, left by Ann Holmes in 1689. At one time the school held 100 children and the average attendance was 64.

Armthorpe school group. On 14 December 1992, the *Doncaster Star* noted that twice in previous years parents and staff had fought and prevented bids to close the school. However, 'Headteacher for the past 19 years Margaret Colbeck now sadly accepted that it was third time unlucky.' Education Authority Chairman Pat Mullany blamed the school closure programme and the Government's insistence that surplus places across the authority's area were removed to save money.

Church Street looking south, with the Wheatsheaf on the left. This pub dates back to at least 1861 when J. Heppenstall was noted as the licensee. A new building was erected in 1928 to the design of Allen & Hickson. Another previous licensee was Richard Stones. Among the previous owners were Septimus Anderson Trustees and Whitworth, Son & Nephew.

Mill Lane showing two farms; Newsome Farm on the left and Mill Farm on the right. John Newsome, after which the farm was named, was a former headmaster at Doncaster Grammar School and an Armthorpe rector. He died in 1708.

Church Street, with Armthorpe church in the distance. The church of Sts Mary and Leonard is chiefly in the perpendicular style, consisting of chancel, nave, north chapel and an octagonal tower and spire. The church was restored in 1886 at a cost of around £1,500, the tower and spire were rebuilt and three new bells were added. In 1888 two stained-glass windows were placed in the church by Lord Auckland. In the chancel are two stained-glass windows, erected by Lord Auckland and Edith Auckland, in 1889. In the nave there is another, erected by the Hon. Agnes and Mary Eden. The west window is a memorial to the Revd E.J. Hayton. The oak reredos was presented to the church by Miss Walbanke Childers. There are two tablets of early date to the Yarborough family. The register dates from 1653.

The junction of Mere Lane and Doncaster Road. Rectory Cottage, on the right, and the building on the left still survive today in this otherwise much altered view where extensive developments have taken place.

A further view of Mill Lane, with Newsome Farm on the left.

Springfield, Armthorpe. A former occupant was Norman Parker.

Scene at Armthorpe.

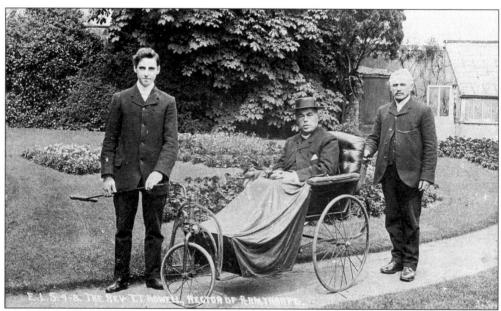

According to his obituary in the *Doncaster Gazette* of 3 February 1911, Revd Thomas Twiss Howell, rector of Armthorpe (seen here in the wheelchair) had been ill for several years. He was educated at St Alban's Hall, Oxford and took his BA in 1875 and MA two years later. For ten years he was the rector of Thorpe, Derbyshire until in 1888 it was announced that he had accepted Mrs Walbanke-Childers' invitation to become rector of Armthorpe. During his time in Armthorpe it was stated that he interested himself in many objects both inside and outside his own parish. He was a very popular man and, when his affliction debarred him from following his duties, deep sympathy was roused.

Woodleigh Cottages.

Nutwell Lane, looking towards Armthorpe village with the Horse and Groom on the left. The pub's owners have included John Winder and Whitworth, Son & Nephew. The pub's existance can be traced back to at least 1852. Among the past licensees were Francis Singleton, Henry Dunks and H. Moverley.

The Mill Lane and Church Street junction. The scene is much altered today; all of the buildings, with the exception of the castellated one on the right, have been demolished.

The Mill Lane and Church Street junction. The two cottages on the left survive today, though in a much altered form.

According to information supplied by A. Dodson to the *Doncaster Evening Post* of 12 July 1982, the parish room was built on Glebe land in 1887 and was endowed with a benefaction of £230 by Miss Selina Walbanke-Childers for church, Sunday school and other church meetings in the first place and as a parish room at the discretion of the rector. The total cost of the building was £450. With the population increase in the late 1920s it was realised that there was a need for a much larger building, so an extension was added. The foundation stone for the extension was laid by Miss Gertrude Bell on 6 September 1930. On 29 November 1930, the new church parish room was opened by Miss Bell. The architects were Allen-Hickson and the builders were Pearson & Blackwell.

The Church Street and Mill Street junction, showing E. Greaves' Cash & Carry Stores.

Armthorpe Follies performing *Beauty and the Beast* during the 1922-23 season.

The first Markham Main Colliery Band, pictured in 1926. The bandmaster is J. Wilson. Also included among those pictured are J.W. Smith and C. Heaton. According to Den Stockley in *Markham Main Colliery Band* (1995): 'Formed in 1925 the MMCB reached championship section status in 1948 having won its way up from the lower grades and remained in that top section until the late 1970s. Sadly, in 1992 the pit closure programme saw the closing of the pit at Armthorpe, but the Band continues as a self-supporting unit – one of just three remaining ex-colliery bands in this area.'

Abercrombie and Johnson, in 1922, said of the Armthorpe Colliery development: 'The new village erected on some of the highest ground available is designed on sound lines, and is sufficiently far away from the colliery to avoid the smoke from the pithead. Full advantage has been taken of the wooded surroundings of the new village site.'

Basil Avenue, Armthorpe, forming part of the colliery village. It was stated in the *Doncaster Chronicle* of 9 May 1924, that when it gets into its full stride the pit will probably provide employment for from 3,000 to 4,000 men: 'The model village when complete, will comprise about 1,000 houses. From 150 to 200 have already been built, and the plans are out for many more. Some 70 acres of land have been acquired for the village, the roads of which will be 24 feet wide, with a nine foot path. The village will be in the form of a semi-circle, and fine avenues of trees being comprised in it. In time Armthorpe will be linked up with Doncaster by one continuous line of dwellings and shops. Armthorpe Lane, the main thoroughfare along which these houses will spring up, is to be greatly widened and improved, a scheme which will involve an expenditure of £42,000 being in contemplation.'

A group of sinkers in a hoppit at Armthorpe's Markham Main. On 6 May 1924 it was announced that the pit sinkers had reached their objective, the famous Barnsley bed of coal. The bed was reached in the No. 1 shaft, at a depth of 727 yards. The pit was, therefore, by no means as deep as some of the other collieries in the Doncaster area. The thickness of the seam was six feet. Markham Main was one of the famous group of Markham pits.

Opposite page, top: Markham Main was the nearest colliery to Doncaster, being only 2 miles from the town centre. It was a pit which worked coal beneath Doncaster Race Course. From the outset, it was considered that another of the local beauty spots would be completely transformed, as the pit was on the fringe of the Sandall Beat woods. Originally, it was anticipated that the Colliery would be sunk by Earl Fitzwilliam. Negotiations were held between him and the Doncaster Corporation for the sale by the latter of their mineral rights under the Town Moor; the conditions of the lease were agreed to, and the consent of the local Government Board obtained. On the basis of the price per foot thick per acre paid by Lord Fitzwilliam, the coal under the Race Common was estimated to be worth something like £450,000 to the town. In the negotiations between the Earl and the Corporation the leasing price agreed upon was £25 per foot of seam per acre, the lease was to apply only to the Barnsley seam. In 1913, however, an announcement was made to the effect that the late Sir Arthur Markham had secured the lease of coal under the land in the Armthorpe, Cantley and Sandall Beat district, belonging to Earl Fitzwilliam and the Doncaster Corporation. Exactly why his Lordship decided, with the consent of the parties concerned, to transfer to Sir Arthur Markham the rights he had acquired never transpired.

Mansfield Crescent, Armthorpe.

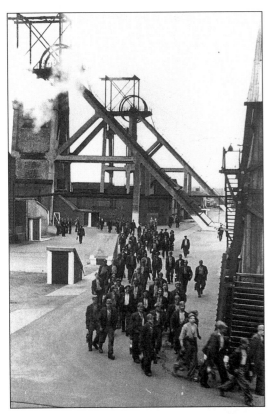

Underground workers at Markham Colliery, leaving the shafts at the end of their shift. No. 1 shaft, the downcast for ventilating the air of mine, is seen behind No. 2, the upcast shaft.

Underground workers *en route* to the lamp cabin at the end of the shift.

Playwright and novelist J.B. Priestley visited Armthorpe's Markham Main on Friday 20 June 1941. The visit formed the subject of his article entitled 'This Problem of Coal', which appeared in the weekly magazine *The Picture Post*. Priestley was accompanied by *Picture Post* photographer Bert Hardy who produced some splendid photographs underground, in the pit yard and round the colliery village. Looking at the article now, it might be regarded as a subtle piece of propaganda.

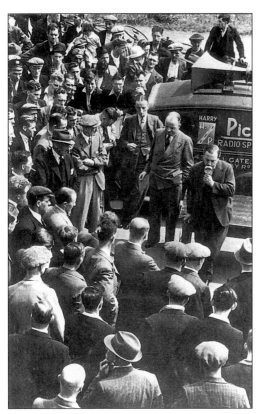

On his arrival in Armthorpe, before visiting the underground workings, Priestley was conducted through the village, which contained almost 1,000 colliery houses. After lunch a pit yard meeting was held and J. Hunter, managing director of the colliery company, introduced Priestley who addressed the miners. Priestley is pictured, with microphone, in the pit yard.

Priestley's account of what he saw provides a unique insight into village life. He said miners invariably lived in their own little communities not far from the pit heads. This meant they were mostly cut off from the general community and almost formed a kind of small separate nation with its own outlook, habits, customs, sympathies and turns of phrase. Preistley is seen here discussing a point with 'Gerry' Margerison at his front gate.

During his visit, Priestley spoke to one managing director who complained bitterly about the lightning strikes in South Yorkshire. In the previous year, it had cost his company some 120,000 tons. Priestley's reaction was: 'Clearly, this will not do. I do not care whose fault it is but we simply cannot afford such luxuries as strikes and lockouts and all other antics of industrial dispute at a time when every ton of coal is urgently required.' Those depicted include, from left to right: 'Prince' (the pony), J.S. Raynor, J. Hunter, J.B. Priestley, T. Baynham, H.J. Humphrys, B. Schofield.

Underground, Priestley was photographed riding on the north east man-haulage, which took him from the pit bottom to north four junction. At the loading point of conveyor 10, north four district, he talked with the loader lads. These were responsible for loading about 800 tubs a shift, each of 16 cwts capacity. Those shown include 'Ike' Carlin (train conductor), J. Hunter, H.J. Humpries, Mr Storey and J.B. Priestley.

When visiting the home of Mr and Mrs Ralph Bell, Priestley was impressed by their young daughter's impromptu tap dancing performance in the back yard. Also seen in the picture is J. Hall, President of the Yorkshire Mineworkers Association.

One particular miner that Priestley met had just finished his shift. He had risen that morning at half past four, had gone underground and hewn out 10 to 11 tons of coal. His snap for the mid-morning snack was a slice or two of bread with a scrape of margarine and a slice of lettuce. After taking a shower at the colliery baths, he had gone home to a dinner of fried potatoes and rice pudding. The miner had not eaten meat since the previous weekend. Numerous miners told Priestley they needed more solid food in order to do their job properly. Their tiny extra meat ration, with the addition of the special cheese allowance, was not good enough.

Preistley said that the Markham colliery village was a good example. Houses were mostly trim outside and nearly always very neat, clean and well cared for inside. There were gardens at the rear and many of the men spent their time working or relaxing in them enjoying the sun and clean air after the heat and darkness 2,000 feet below.

Priestley, at the loading point of conveyor 10, north four district, talks with the loader lads.

Doncaster Central MP, Harold Walker (third from the right), is pictured during a visit to Markham Main. The colliery survived until 1996.

Two
Hatfield and
Hatfield Woodhouse

Hatfield High Street, looking towards the junction with Station Road, *c.* 1950. The Doncaster Co-op's Hatfield branch can be seen in the distance, while the Bay Horse Inn (on the right) proudly displays a sign for Darley's ales. Within the sign is the brewery's symbol for good ale. (Photograph by Reg Elliff.)

Two views showing Hatfield church (St Lawrence, formerly St Mary). The one above is seen from Cuckoo Lane. The view below is seen from Station Road, with Cuckoo Lane in the distance. Westfield House, a two-storey building with a pantiled roof, is to the left and Church Lodge is to the right, carrying a date stone which is inscribed 1711. John Magilton in his *The Doncaster District an Archaeological Survey* (1977) describes the church as a: 'Large cruciform church with Norman elements, including both aisles. The crossing tower is Tudor. Nave arcades are early thirteenth century and other details are Perp. An impressive building for a village.' The church was restored in 1873 and this work, together with further restorations, continued up to 1891, costing £2,017 altogether. The north chantry chapel, partially burnt on Easter day in 1887, was thoroughly restored. There are sittings for 450 persons. The parish registers date from 1566 and, up to the end of 1777 are written on parchment, from that date on they are recorded on paper.

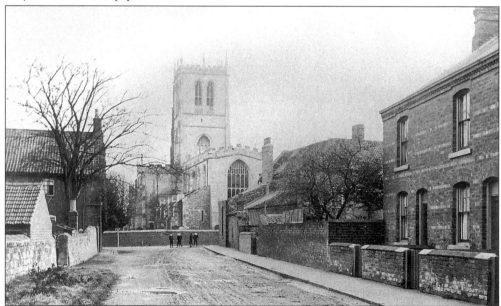

High Street looking east, with the Ingram Arms Hotel on the left. The picture was taken when A. Squires was the licensee. The hotel dates from at least 1855 and past owners have included the Hon. Mrs Meynell Ingram and Whitworth, Son & Nephew. The premises were rebuilt during 1923 and the present owners are John Smiths. Only the group of properties off-centre, to the right, still exist.

Looking along Station Road with High Street to the right. The group of properties on the left includes Corban House. Grocer and seedsman George Marsdin's shop, on the left, was later occupied by a branch of the Doncaster Co-operative Society. The house to the right has since been demolished.

Station Road facing Manor Road, *c.* 1908. Kelly's West Riding Yorkshire Directory of that year stated: 'Hatfield is a parish, township and large and pleasant village, and is near the navigable river Don and the canal which runs through the village of Stainforth and on the Doncaster and Thorne Road, 7 miles north east from Doncaster, 3 south west from Thorne and 165 from London; it is in the Doncaster division of the Riding...' The buildings on the right include Hawthorne House. The buildings on the left, up to the Blue Bell, have been demolished to create a car park for the pub.

High Street looking east showing the Ingram Arms Hotel (left) when T. Hart was the licensee. The *Doncaster Chronicle* of 27 February 1936 mentioned that a well known Hatfield character 'Jack Hawley', or Lionel Scott Pilkington (his correct name), often rode into the kitchen of the old Ingram Arms Hotel on his pony, calling for a brandy for himself and a pint of beer for the pony. Several buildings seen on both sides of the street have since been cleared.

View of High Street and Manor Road with the Blue Bell Inn, off centre to the right, and the old court house – an eighteenth-century brick building with a central pediment.

High Street and Manor Road, facing the junction with Station Road. The Blue Bell Inn is on the right, and at this time William Maxwell held the license. The pub's existence can be traced back to at least 1788. Among the former owners were Thomas Tune, and James Fox & Sons Ltd.

High Street, *c.* 1910. At the time the picture was taken, by Doncaster-based photographer Edgar Leonard Scrivens, Hatfield was gas lit by a limited liability company. Note the gas lamp on the left.

High Street, seen in the days before the problems caused by unloading noise and the fumes and vibrations of heavy traffic, as it trundles through on the A18.

Two views of High Street looking east. The Bay Horse Inn is the main feature above. The pub dates from at least 1787. A former owner was William Marsden Darley. At the West Riding Brewster Sessions held during March 1937, magistrates granted a new license to replace the one held by the Bay Horse. This was because of a proposed new road. In the event neither the new pub nor the road were built. Partially seen on the right is the frontage of the Red Lion, which closed in 1908. On the left, below, locals are posing outside draper and grocer, Joseph Clarke's business premises. The gentleman himself stands to the left of the car.

Two further views of High Street. The building on the right in the top picture has since been demolished. *Hatfield in History* (1970) Derek Holland ed., mentions: 'The old core of Hatfield is a "street village", with farmhouses along either side of the street, some with their axes parallel to the street and a few with their gables to the street. At the rear are usually farm buildings and outhouses, all the buildings (including the house itself) stand on a plot of land known as a "toft". Behind all the tofts and parallel to the village street ran a back lane, and this still exists on the south side of the village, running eastwards from the side of the Blue Bell.'

Hatfield High Street. The Limes (No. 24) is on the left. The property where the workmen can be seen has since been demolished and forms part of the library site. In the picture below, the old property, up to the row of terraced houses, has been redeveloped.

A plan to by-pass Hatfield's High Street, seen here, was illustrated in the *Doncaster Chronicle* of 3 February 1938. The new road was to leave the A18, near the Don Valley Brewery, cut across the New Mill Field, and then rejoin the thoroughfare, close to the chapel on Back Field Lane. Magilton (in the 1977 publication) claims that the cottages on the right are in some ways Hatfield's most interesting group of buildings: 'Renovated eighteenth century, but almost certainly timber-framed.'

High Street, looking west, with the Lymes on the left. Over the last hundred years, many changes have taken place along the thoroughfare in both its social structure and the size of its population. But, it has been noted (*Hatfield in History*, 1970) that its earlier characteristics are still visible in the buildings, falling into three categories: the larger houses, the farmhouses, and smaller houses and cottages.

Hatfield High Street looking towards Thorne. Victoria Hall is out of view to the right.

Two views of Ash Hill, noted as one of Hatfield's most picturesque areas. Since the Second World War much private housing development has occurred around the area. Ash Hill House, a brick building which has since been converted to a restaurant, is featured in both pictures..

High Street, when traffic on the road was infrequent. During the post-war years, sections of the street gave way to new housing developments. A further change is that a large percentage of the thoroughfare's population do not work in the village as they once did.

High Street looking towards Thorne, with No. 62 High Street on the right. The house in the distance has since been demolished. The agricultural machinery travelling along High Street accurately reflects the era, with trade directories for this period noting over forty farmers in the Hatfield area.

Broom Lodge, an eighteenth-century, two-storey building with an attic. The property was once occupied by Col. Charles Frederick Hoyle.

The Grange, a two-storey pantiled, brick building. Magillton (1977) states that modern notice claims a date of 1717, but the majority of building looks to be of a later date.

Hatfield House, which was demolished in 1955.

The Manor House is aptly described in *Hatfield in History* (1970) Derek Holland ed.: 'The Manor House itself really calls for separate treatment: it is the largest house in the village and its inhabitants originally occupied a special place in the community's social and economic structure. Nothing now remains visible of the Saxon and medieval Royal palaces, nor even of the timber-framed building which Leland described in the early sixteenth century…It would appear that the present L-shaped building was rebuilt in the late seventeenth century, and that further renovations were carried out in the early eighteenth century.'

Hatfield Carnival moving along High Street in 1923. Both the bride and groom (pictured towards the bottom right) were men – Stanley Fidler and Robert Baker. According to the sign being held by the person in the centre, the musicians depicted belong to the Balby Bridge Novelty Band.

High Street, looking east, showing some interesting modes of transport.

Looking back towards the Ingram Arms with sadler, Charles Gravil's business premises on the right. The property is currently occupied by a chiropodist. Some properties on the right have since been removed, making way for an entrance to Ivy Close. Other tradespeople to be found in Hatfield at the time of the picture, around 1910, included boot makers, blacksmiths, wheelwrights, market gardeners, and ironmongers.

View from Old Epworth Road with Trundle Cottage on the right.

High Street featuring the Red Lion public house on the right. At the West Riding Brewster Sessions held during March 1908, the pub's license was objected to on the grounds of redundancy. Sergeant Ripley, giving evidence, said the Red Lion was a beer house and was only 33 yards from the Bay Horse. In his opinion a license for the house was unnecessary for the requirements of the district. He did not consider it was well lit, the bedrooms were very poor and the house was bad for police supervision. The building which includes Avondale and Ryecroft is on the right. There is a date stone inscribed 1882 in the centre of the building.

High Street featuring the Victoria Hall on the right. The building carries a date stone inscribed 1901. The *Doncaster Gazette* of 31 October 1946 mentions: 'The Victoria Hall which was used for Civil Defence purposes during the war, is the scene of dancing about once a fortnight.'

Garden fête at Hatfield Vicarage. The building, in light grey bricks, dates from around 1870. The original cost was about £450, and later additions were made to the rear of the house. Kelly (1927) states: 'The living is a vicarage, net yearly value £300, with residence, in the gift of H.R.R. Coventry esq…'

Boys at Ryecroft Boarding School, which was run by Mr and Mrs Crate. Mr Crate was also a tutor to the Chetwynd family at Wyndthorpe Hall, situated nearby.

The rebuilt Ingram Arms public house is on the right. Shortly before the work took place the *Doncaster Gazette* of 31 August 1923 said: 'The Ingram Arms, a house familiar to many travellers through the main street of Hatfield, is to be rebuilt and very considerably improved in respect to accommodation and modern equipment, by a Doncaster firm of contractors, Messrs Dennis Gill & Son. The architects, Messrs Allen & Hickson of Doncaster, have prepared a scheme for reconstruction…The old hotel occupies a commanding site. It was named after the Ingram family, who were esteemed in the Hatfield district, and the head of whose house became Lord of the Manor of Hatfield in the seventeenth century…The new Hotel is designed on the lines of the Tudor style of architecture…'

Almshouses on Doncaster Road, built by Thomas Goodworth of Doncaster in 1914.

High Street looking towards the junction with Station Road, with the Doncaster Co-operative Society's premises – branch no. 11 is in the distance. On the right is Hatfield post office, seen at a time when it was occupied by J.T. Hopkinson. (Photographed by Reg Elliff.)

Cutting the first sod at Hatfield Main – which was actually over the parish boundary in Stainforth. The Hatfield Colliery Co. was formed towards the end of 1910, but it was not until Thursday 4 October 1911 that the first sod of the new colliery was formally cut, and the sinking proper did not begin till 1912. At the sod cutting ceremony it was said (*Doncaster Chronicle* 5 October 1911) that: 'Shortly after half past twelve in the afternoon Thomas Townrow, of Chesterfield, chairman of the directors of the company stood in the centre of the ring which marked the spot where number one shaft is to be sunk, and with a brand new small digging spade he cut the turf in an oblong, and putting his spade beneath it, turned it over. Mr Townrow then went to the other shaft site, followed by the company [of other officals] and performed a similar operation.'

Preliminary work at Hatfield Colliery. The *Doncaster Chronicle* of 5 March 1915 noted that it was impossible to visit Hatfield without being impressed with the changes that were coming over the scene: 'Here we have a district, once the happy hunting ground of Kings and Monarchs, now destined to become a centre of coal and commerce. On the spot where royalty once disported themselves, where archers drew the long bow and sent their shafts at the red deer, are now shafts of a very different character, up which the latest machinery will wind coal from the bowels of the earth.'

Pit sinkers at Hatfield Colliery. On 9 April 1915 the *Doncaster Chronicle* reported that a sad fatality at the colliery, had broken the record of almost complete immunity from serious accidents which the pit had enjoyed. At about 1.30 p.m. on Tuesday 6 April, Frederick Creswell, of No. 1 Thorne Road, Stainforth, a pit sinker aged 32 years, was at the bottom of No. 1 shaft with 17 other sinkers. They had sent a full hoppit to the surface, and shortly afterwards the empty one descended. By some means this caught Creswell on the head. The hoppit knocked him down and rolled him over; he was shockingly injured and was apparently killed on the spot.

Worker at Hatfield Colliery.

Construction work on some of the buildings at Hatfield Colliery. In March 1915 it was reported that the progress of the work had been a good deal affected by the war. Employment for at least fifty per cent more sinkers could have been found since the war started. At that time 130 sinkers were employed out of a total workforce of 300 men who were working at the pit. The war had meant the withdrawal of a number of men. It had also affected the supply of material.

Giving a report on the progress at Hatfield Colliery the *Doncaster Chronicle* of 21 March 1912 stated: 'Both shafts have now been sunk through the running sand, and the permanent shaft lining has been completed. This consists of reinforced concrete which is being used, so it is said, for the first time in this country. The headgear for one of the shafts is now being erected, and when this is finished the other will be commenced. The depth is now about 15 yards. The permanent chimney, 180 feet high, is now built, and six Lancashire boilers have been set.'

Hatfield Main Colliery which, in 1927, was acquired by the Carlton Main Colliery Company. At that time the colliery employed 2,300 men and the daily output was 2,400 tons.

Hatfield Main Colliery was well situated on the communications network, being close to a LNER railway line and the Stainforth & Keadby Canal.

Scene at Hatfield Colliery. There was a Social Section at the Colliery (*Hatfield in History*, 1970), which arranged concerts and lectures for the workers. The Workers' Educational Association was also active in organizing adult classes. For example, in the year 1937-38, there were four WE classes in Stainforth, with a total of fifty-six students.

Interior view at Hatfield Colliery. At one time the Hatfield Main Colliery Co. Ltd controlled royalties extending over 14,000 acres in Hatfield and the neighbouring parishes of Stainforth, Barnby Dun and Fishlake.

Workmen at Hatfield Colliery.

Interior view at Hatfield Colliery. By 1930, the colliery employed around 3,600 men. It was part of a group of collieries that between them produced six million tons of coal annually.

Hatfield Colliery was closed during the mid-1990s after a review meeting. It was one of the last outposts of South Yorkshire's coalfields. The closure affected hundreds of families in the Stainforth and Hatfield areas. However, shortly afterwards it was announced that a management buyout team had been granted a fifteen year lease to run the colliery.

View of Hatfield Colliery.

A side view of Hatfield Main locomotive no. 4 on 23 October 1954. (Photographed by Geoff Warnes.)

Broadway, Dunscroft, Hatfield which is over a mile long. Dunscroft, a mile away from Hatfield and the same distance from the colliery, was one of the areas developed to house the colliers. *Hatfield in History* (1970) notes: 'By 1930 there were 1,471 colliery houses which had been built by the colliery owners, and most of these were fitted with bathrooms.'

The Village School, Hatfield Woodhouse, *c.* 1908. This was erected, with master's house, in 1877, at a cost of £864. It was enlarged in 1894 to cater for 120 children. The average attendance at the time of the picture was 76. Walter G. Warwick was the master and Mrs Warwick the mistress.

Hatfield Woodhouse was once described as a straggling village, one and a half miles south east of Hatfield. During the early part of the present century over twenty farmers were noted as living in the area. Pictured here is a brushseller, known locally as 'Old George', with his pony, Dolly. The other figures are Mrs Fiddler with her daughters, Alice and Mary.

A Hatfield Woodhouse school group, *c.* 1903. Included among those pictured is Thomas Cragg who won a Military Medal during the First World War.

A Hatfield Woodhouse school group, thought to be pictured during the 1920s. The teacher is Miss Tomlinson, who later became Mrs Watts – wife of a Thorne dentist. Children from several noted Hatfield Woodhouse families are depicted, including the Harpers and the Drurys.

Interestingly, in March 1935, Hatfield Woodhouse Parish Council decided, by sixteen votes to three, to seek powers to provide a supply of water to the parish. The water supply at that time was obtained from wells. Headmaster J. Thompson, in criticizing the village water supplies said that by courtesy of his wife the 250 children at his school used the pump supply in his yard. Thompson added that he had never drunk a drop of water for five years without boiling it. The children were drinking the water out of buckets. Mr E. Plumstead said that worms 'a foot long' came out of the pumps!

A view of Hatfield Woodhouse by Doncaster-based photographer, Edgar Leonard Scrivens.

The Spotted Bull public house, when William Bottom junior was the licensee. The pub can be traced back to at least 1830 and the license was referred for compensation during 1909. One of the former owners was Susannnah Wilburn. Among the licensees were George Hepworth and Thomas Wilburn.

The Spotted Bull is on the left. The post office is the central building on the left, Joseph Draper may have been the sub-postmaster at this time. Letters received through Doncaster arrived about 7.50 a.m. and 6.30 p.m. and were despatched at 9.45 a.m. and 7.10 p.m. There was no Sunday delivery.

Low Street, Hatfield Woodhouse. Magilton (1977) observes: 'There is no indication from the street plan or surviving property boundaries that Woodhouse was ever anything more than a late collection of brick farmhouses with no real nucleus.'

View with the Wesleyan Methodist chapel on the right.

The Green Tree Inn at the junction. The picture was taken during the period when Ellen Brown was the licensee. The inn dates back to at least 1822. Former owners of the premises included William Hepworth and Charles Proctor.

Low Street, Hatfield Woodhouse, featuring the Ebeneezer chapel on the right, built in 1858. The building was demolished in September 1967, being replaced by another structure that was completed a year later.

Kelly (1908) stated that Slay Pits at Hatfield Woodhouse, seen here: 'consists of two farms and five small tenements, half a mile east [of Hatfield].'

MARRIED WOMEN'S RACE · HATFIELD WOODHOUSE SHOW.

Competitors in the Married Women's Race at Hatfield Woodhouse Show are captured in full flight.

View of Hatfield Woodhouse. It has been suggested that the motor vehicle, seen in the distance on the right, may belong to photographer Edgar Leonard Scrivens, who took this picture.

The Wesleyan chapel, built in Bawtry Road during 1825. G. Morris in *The Story of Methodism in Doncaster & District 1743-1988* (1988) mentions that: 'Many of these village chapels consisted of only one room, with an iron stove for heating, and candles or oil lamps for lighting, and would seat 30 to 40 people.' The chapel was demolished during the late 1960s.

Three
Stainforth

Emmerson Avenue, with The Savoy Cinema on the right. The premises, accommodating more than 800 patrons, were built in 1922 by Frederick Hopkinson & Co. Ltd to the designs of L. Hopkinson. By 1956 it was owned by Star Cinemas (London) Ltd, but had closed down by the end of the decade.

Keel on the canal at Stainforth. Note the young children near the mast. In *Stainforth Official Guide* (*c.* 1925), it was stated that the canal offered great possibilities – cheap transport to Sheffield and intermediate stations on the one hand, and to the Trent, the Humber, Hull, and the North Sea Ports on the other. In addition the canal being joined to the Aire and Calder canal offered direct communication with Leeds and other cities.

On the canal at Stainforth. In 1793 an Act of Parliament was passed to make a navigable canal from the Don at Stainforth to the Trent at Keadby. This canal was completed and opened around 1802. In 1837 the Stainforth and Keadby Canal was sold, under powers of an Act of Parliament, to the proprietors of the Doncaster Navigation Company who extended it to Doncaster and Sheffield.

View of the canal with the East Bank on the left and the South Bank on the right. Shipbuilding at Stainforth commenced during the nineteenth century and a very successful business was built up. The yards were on the banks of the canal. The area, of moderate size, included a dry dock for repair work and had upon it workshops, timber storage sheds, a saw room, and other utilities. The principal kind of boats constructed here were keels suitable for canal work and other small craft.

The Sheffield and South Yorkshire Canal, running 43 miles from Keadby to Sheffield, used to carry working sailing craft known as the Humber keels and sloops. These boats, anything up to 75 feet long, were first made from the hulls of oak, later of iron, then steel. The keel boats started working the rivers of Yorkshire as early as the fourteenth century, and continued under sail until shortly after the end of the Second World War. Powered by a single square sail – or if there was no wind, pulled by men or horses – they carried timber, coal, food gravel...anything that was needed, between the ports and inland farms and factories. The Humber sloop, with a sail before and after the mast, was more manoeuvrable than the keel, and was better suited to river and coast work. The row of white cottages at the centre of the picture has since been demolished.

The Old Bridge, Stainforth.

The canal at Stainforth, looking east. In E. White's Trade Directory of 1837 Stainforth is described as having a spacious quay with cranes and other conveniences for a considerable number of sloops of which many belong to the inhabitants. N. Barrass in *Stainforth – Our Heritage* (1986) adds: 'The crane then mentioned is still remembered as being located on the East Bank, built there to handle the heavy leeboards, anchor and mast, along with any other surplus weight no longer required by the vessels on their journey inland. On their return the necessary gear would again be taken on board…'

View from the West Bank, featuring the Black Swan Inn, off centre to the right. The pub may be traced back to 1749 when it was named the 'Bridge Inn'. It was subsequently titled the 'Swan' and later the 'Black Swan'. Although the local licensing registers state that the license was not renewed in 1891, the inn is still noted in Doncaster Gazette Directory of 1893. The building survived, being used for a time as a lodging house, until around 1960.

The communities at Thorne and Stainforth knew how to relax as well as work, and the annual regattas were a source of great entertainment for both participants and spectators. The events mainly took place during feast week, which was held in late September. At the turn of the century the Hon Edward Frederick Lindley Wood, of Temple Newsam, Leeds, was the Lord of the Manor. The trustees of the B.P. Broomhead were the chief landowners, most of the rest of the land being in the hands of small holders. The population in 1901 was 735.

John S. Porter's business premises. In one of his advertisements he claimed that he could supply any kind of motor car. He was an agent for Raleigh, BSA and Hercules motor cycles and cycles. In the ironmongery side of the business Porter supplied fireplaces, felting, netting, mangles, household utensils, and all kinds of hardware.

Well known local character, Isaac Henry Bowling, on the left, started his butcher's business on Field Road during 1892. In the background is Isaac's shop, and his home, Chapel Field House. Fritz Bowling is on the right.

A further view of Bowling's shop on Field Road. Manager Billy Fowler is on the left, Fritz Bowling is the motorcyclist and Fred Birdsey is on the right, adjacent to the British Legion's hut. A butchery business still thrives in Bowling's premises today.

Looking along Thorne Road. In 1885, Stainforth became a parish in its own right, breaking away from Hatfield. Therefore the parish church of St Matthew, built in 1819, instead of being a chapel-of-ease, dependent on the mother church, became a separate entity.

Silver Street with the Primitive Methodist chapel on the right, built in 1870. Prior to this, services were held in East Lane. The building closed around 1970. Barrass (1986) stated that the parish church, along with the two Methodist chapels 'were mainly the hub of activities around which life in the community once centred.'

Stainforth junction signal box. In 1856, the Stainforth and Keadby Navigation proprietors laid down rail lines on the banks of their own canal from Doncaster to Thorne, and for a time shipped coal on board vessels from a drop at Thorne Lock. In 1859, they carried the rails to Keadby. In 1866, the MS&L Railway constructed a new line from Doncaster to Thorne, Barnetby, and so on and the traffic from the old canal line was immediately diverted to it. The line was acquired in 1901 by the Great Central Railway Company and later the LNER.

Looking towards Stainforth and Hatfield Station.

The Station Inn on the canal bank dates from at least 1867. Prior to this date, the premises may have been called the Mariner's Compass, or Compass extending back to 1812. Past owners have included the River Dun Co. and the Worksop & Retford Brewery Co. The inn closed around 1960 and was demolished along with the building once occupied by the Black Swan. Barrass (1986) states: 'In their stead the Peacock and the Harvester, the first public houses to be built in the village since the King George Hotel of the early 1920s.'

Scene along Station Road. The Stainforth Official Guide (c. 1925) noted: 'Although Stainforth is of undoubted antiquity, it cannot boast of any really ancient historical landmark. The origin of Stainforth dates back to Saxon times. De La Pryme (1670-1704), the local historian, in his MSS history, states: "This little town in ye Saxon Stanford, which signifies stony-ford, so called from a ford of that nature that is here over the River Don, which is passable on horseback in summer time, but are forced in winter to use ye boats.'"

Briers Lane with the Wesleyan Methodist chapel in the distance on the left. The chapel was built in 1820, with a Sunday schoolroom being added two years later. The building had seating for 164 people.

Members of Stainforth Labour Party's women's section are pictured outside the British Legion Club on Field Road.

Thorne Road, looking towards Thorne.

Street scene at Stainforth. On Friday 11 September 1925, the *Doncaster Chronicle* reported: 'Last Tuesday was a proud day [for Stainforth], and especially for its Parish Council. It marks the fruition of a scheme inaugurated last March, and which has resulted in Stainforth being the first township on the Thorne side of Doncaster to have its streets so lighted. The Stainforth streets were officially lighted for the first time at 8.30 on Tuesday night, the scheduled lighting up time, by Mr Whiteley, the Chairman of the Stainforth Parish Council...'

The vehicle fleet of Stainforth coal merchants Redgard Bros, pictured near Millcroft House *c.* 1933. The business was set up by brothers Harold and Jack Redgard, who hailed from Derbyshire, in the 1920s. Shortly afterwards however, Jack left and another brother, Arthur joined the firm. In the early days, Redgards transported coal from Hatfield Colliery to the tippler along the canal. They also ran charabancs and later branched out into the building trade when the coal business was slack during the summer months. The business ceased to trade around the mid-1960s. From left to right are: Harold Redgard, Arthur Redgard, Alf Johnson, ? Crossley.

Draper, S. Ward's business premises.

Two views of the Fox Inn, situated on Field Road. The pub can be traced back to at least 1822. The past owners include Elizabeth Kelham, and Hewitt Bros Ltd. The premises were altered in 1912.

Hatfield Main Club on East Lane. Hatfield Colliery may be seen in the distance.

The King George Hotel, Church Road, which opened on Tuesday 5 December 1922. The hotel was built by Messrs Frederick Hopkinson & Co. (Worksop), Ltd, from the designs of Frederick Hopkinson. The same firm was also responsible for erecting Rossington's Royal Hotel. There was no formal opening ceremony at Stainforth, but J. Farnsworth, licensee of the Royal, came over to represent the owner, Frederick Robinson, who was unable to be present, and H.N. Berry and J. Walker were present from Hatfield Main Colliery. The villagers were the guests of the owner at night. The license holder was Charles Edwin Lister, who was in the Royal Munster Fusiliers for eighteen years.

The *Doncaster Chronicle* of 11 September 1925, noted: 'The whole of the houses in Stainforth are being supplied with electricity for lighting, heating, and general domestic purposes by Electrial Distribution of Yorkshire Ltd, and arrangements have been made for dealing similarly with a further 800 houses, making over 1,300 in all now in course of erection in the same district.'

The Public Benefit Boot Co.'s premises are on the left in this street scene.

During the 1920s Stainforth expanded considerably, especially along the Hatfield roads, because of the developments which took place at the Hatfield Main Colliery. Several hundred houses were built in the town. The Thorne Rural District Council built 300 houses, the Colliery Co. built 1,471, and Messrs Porter built 200, in addition to a large number put up by private builders. The scene here is on Church Road looking towards Stanley Gardens.

Field Road with the Fox public house in the distance. Barrass (1986) sets the scene at the time of the colliery and housing developments: 'Numerous tales could be told of those arriving on the scene to take up employment at the new colliery heralded by the engineers and the pit sinkers, as work progressed their numbers swelled. In many cases the breadwinners came here alone, living in lodgings until security for the future was established, then sending for the remainder of the family to join them in creating a new life in strange surroundings.'

View looking along East Lane, stretching from Station Road to the Field Road, Silver Street and Thorne Road junction. The is one of several views of Stainforth taken by Reg Elliff, whose business premises were in Balby.

Woodcock's shop (left) on Bridge Hill/Water Lane. The Stainforth Guide (*c.* 1925) mentioned: 'Stainforth is well looked after medically, there are several medical practitioners resident in Stainforth and District. The town has its own Nursing Association. Employees of the Colliery Company, paying each week to the funds of the Doncaster Royal Infirmary, are able to obtain free treatment there.'

Looking along Doncaster road with the market and Poplar House in the distance. Pictured among the buildings on the left are Fern Cottages and 'Douthwaite'. Of Stainforth and its market: 'It was made a market and a fair town by King Edward ye third at the request of Edward, Duke of York, into whom the King had given this town amongst the rest that belonged to the late Earl of Warren, so that this town flourished mightily then and became very rich, for besides its market, which was frequented by a great number of traders, there landed here all those trafficking men that came from the Isle of Axholme, from Thorne, and other places that were every Saturday were bound for Doncaster market, for they never went higher up the river than the town...'

Scene along Church Road with F. Mumby's shop on the left. Other traders include C. Fowler and H.S. Parkin (dispensing and photographic chemist).

Station Road with Powell's florists on the left. Among the other traders are Dexters and David Haigh. Stainforth's early closing day was each Wednesday. At one time buses from all the neighbouring towns and villages – Doncaster, Kirk Sandall, Barnby Dun, Fishlake, Sykehouse, Thorne, Moorends, Goole, Hatfield and Dunscroft – all converged in Stainforth.

Church Road with the market and Poplar House in the distance on the right. The police station, on the left, was erected by the West Riding County Council, with a detached house for the resident sergeant and two semi-detached houses for police constables. Kelly's 1927 Directory notes John William Naylor as the sergeant in charge, with five constables.

The Wesleyan chapel on the right, including hall and school was opened on 5 November 1925, at a cost of nearly £10,000. The chapel and school provided seating for 450 people and 400 scholars respectively. The building, of Accrington bricks with stone dressings, was constructed under the South Yorkshire Coal Field Mission Scheme, and was of the type erected in Denaby and other districts. Messrs Johnson & Moore, of Balby, were the builders and Messrs Gelder & Kitchen of Hull, the architects.

To take this picture, the photographer has stood in Hall Road and pointed his camera towards the Silver Street and Finkle Street junction. The sign on the property in the distance advertises the business of L. Millsom & Son. The rear of the Fox Inn is on the right. The large house beyond has since been demolished.

Station Road, captured by local photographers James Simmonton & Sons. Among the businesses are H. Wright, The Tobacco Shop, Moderne Salons and Melias. Among the other traders once noted along the route were fried fish merchants, confectioners, butchers, newsagents and boot manufacturers. Since the time of the picture, much re-development has taken place in the area.

Station Road by Reg Elliff. The businesses along the thoroughfare include those of S. & H. Morris Ltd, R.C. Hopkinson Ltd, Jackson Ltd, Modern Salons and Melias.

Four

Thorne

The water pump in Thorne Market Place. The pump was erected after the Crimean War. In the background is the Doncaster Mutual Co-operative Society's building. Kelly (1908) said: 'Thorne is a parish, small market and union town and head of a county court district…and is 10 miles north east from Doncaster. The River Don flows about a mile north-west of the town, and the Stainforth and Keady canal passes on the south, giving access to the Trent. The town is lighted with gas from works established in 1837 and belonging to a private company. The trade of keel building is carried on here. The Market Day is Wednesday. The Hon Edward F. Lindley Wood, of Temple Newsam Leeds is Lord of the Manor.'

Market Place featuring, in the background, the business premises of Barnes Bros milliners and drapers. Magilton (1977) commented: 'The small market town [of Thorne] contains a number of buildings of interest and at least three important archaeological sites are known. In particular, the group of buildings on the Market Place deserves mention and forms an essential part of the modern townscape.'

Market Place looking towards Silver Street. In the background are the premises of H. Reid (grocer), E.W. Pidd (pork butcher), J.W. Hirst (ironmonger) and G. Harrison (butcher).

Both aspects of Market Place show W. Wrigleys printing office. According to his obituary in the *Doncaster Chronicle* of 10 April 1931, Wrigley had been the proprietor of a printing business and stationer's shop in the Market Place for a number of years and had lived in Thorne for over half a century. He was born in Keadby in 1853, and came to Thorne when he was thirteen. He was apprenticed to the late Joseph Mason who owned the business that was later to become Wrigley's, and which subsequently became the property of his son. For a short time he was away from Thorne, working in Huddersfield. When Mason died, he took over the business from his widow. The Red Lion can also be seen in the bottom picture.

Market Place looking down Silver Street, with the Co-op on the right and the Green Dragon public house in the centre of the picture. Thorne has held its market charter since 1658. This also gave the town the right to stage two fairs annually. Kelly (1927) states: 'The market day is Wednesday. Thorne agricultural show is largely attended and is held, the cattle fair on the first Tuesday after June 11, the agricultural show on Wednesday and the gala and fireworks on Thursday, after the show. A cattle fair is also held on the first Monday and Tuesday after October 11.'

Market Place. The vehicle in the centre may belong to Edgar Leonard Scrivens, who took the picture. Note also the charabanc on the left.

Market Place looking towards Church Street and St Nicholas's church. At the entrance to Church Street, the premises of William Hallgarth (patent medicine vendor) and George Lester (hairdresser) can be seen.

Market Place and the White Hart Hotel. The date on the building relates to renovation work which took place in 1737. It does not refer to the construction or opening date of the premises. J. Webster was the White Hart's licensee at the time of the picture. To the right, at the entrance to King Street, are the business premises of Frederick Hattersley (grocer) and Benjamin G. Platt (boot maker).

Canal Bridge and South Parade, in the distance. In a short article entitled 'Bridges in the Doncaster District,' the *Doncaster Chronicle* of 14 August 1931 noted that the old toll-bar bridge over the canal at Thorne 'has been taken down and replaced by a structure of concrete and iron, suitable for heavier motor traffic, but so little wider that in that respect it has little advantages over the old wooden bridge which impeded traffic for so many years.' The Canal Tavern can be traced back to at least 1822, and the former owners have included the River Dun Co. Ltd. At the time of the picture Percy Kellitt was the licensee.

The Locks, Thorne, on the Stainforth & Keady canal. At one time the South Yorkshire Railway ran virtually alongside the canal at this point. John Platt in *Thorne's First Railway* (1991) states: 'The single-track line [from Strawberry Island, north of Doncaster, to Thorne] was built by contractors Blyth of Conisbrough, and the first train, which consisted of 10 coal trucks, arrived at Thorne Lock shortly after 12 noon on Tuesday 11 December 1855.'

The swing bridge over the canal at Thorne Lock, looking south east. Mike Taylor in *Memories of Sheffield & South Yorkshire Navigation* (1988) explains that by the dawn of the twentieth century, the Sheffield Canal, Don Navigation, Stainforth & Keadby Canal (part of which is seen here) and Dearne & Dove Canal had merged to become the Sheffield & South Yorkshire Navigation, forming a direct link between Sheffield and Keadby and the River Trent, with a branch (the Dearne & Dove Canal) from Swinton to the Barnsley Canal.

Pashley or Wike Bridge, looking east along the canal at Southend, Thorne. The bridge keeper's house on the left has since been demolished and another property has been erected nearby.

The swing bridge at Thorne, connecting South Parade and Kirton Lane/Hatfield Road. A fly-over now carries traffic over the canal. Laurie Thorp in *Thorne Great Bridge* (1993) details the construction of a new stone bridge near this point in 1752, over the River Dunn.

Locks at Thorne, facing south east. Dunstan's yard is on the left.

The canal locks at Thorne facing south east. On the right is the shipyard of Messrs Dunstan Ltd, which was established at Thorne about 1854. Richard Dunstan, the founder, transferred his rope making and ship rigging business from Torksey, near Lincoln, to Thorne. Soon after settling in Thorne, he saw the possibility for barge building and started the industry for which Thorne became so well known. During the 1920s, the Dunstan shipyard covered three acres, and there were nine berths for barges up to 300 tons capacity.

The canal at Thorne, looking towards Thorne Locks with Dunstan's yard to the right.

Thorne Waterside, formerly a hamlet and port, lies about a mile north west of the town centre on the River Don. Magilton (1977) states: 'This hamlet is now isolated from Thorne itself by the M18 motorway…[It] is in many respects a fossilized survivor of the nineteenth century…Waterside's great days of prosperity were in the late eighteenth and early nineteenth centuries. In the distance is the site that was formerly occupied by an oil cake works, which closed around 1930. The *Doncaster Chronicle* of 8 February 1962 reported: '…perhaps most symbolic of the lingering death of Waterside is the now reed-strewn bed of the River Don. As one turns off the Selby Road and walks up the narrow lane to Waterside, the bend of the river that once gave mercantile prosperity to the village looms up revealing its muddy and littered bed.'

On the canal at Thorne, looking towards Thorne Lock. On the left is part of Staniland's boatyard.

Upper Kenyon Street, looking towards Lower Kenyon Street, by Edgar Leonard Scrivens, who took many pictures of Thorne. During the early part of the present century, Thorne's principal landowners included the Trustees of Makin Durham esq; James Elmhurst esq JP; John Chester Coulman esq JP; and John Henry Bletcher.

St Nicholas Road, Thorne, extending from North Eastern Road to Church Street. The house on the left is Hillcrest, the one in the distance is St Nicholas' Lodge.

101

Two views of Northfields (now called King Edward Road), extending between the town centre and the road to Moorends. Kelly (1908) notes the following private residents of Northfield: Revd George Craig Anderson, Miss Atkinson, George Elland, Richard Forster, John Green, Mrs Lynas, Miss Methley, Charles Sanderson, Mrs Spencer and James W. Spoforth. The obituary of C.W. Darley, brewery owner, in the *Doncaster Chronicle* of 25 June 1926 notes that he was also a Northfield resident.

Fieldside, showing Darley's brewery with its towering chimney in the distance. On 12 June 1992, the *Doncaster Star* reported: 'The Darley's brewery chimney, which was a Thorne landmark for more than a century could have collapsed at any time, demolition experts have revealed. A crack ran the full length of the 200 ft structure and had made the structure unsafe. But it still took two pounds of explosives to bring the old chimney crashing down in a cloud of dust, with hundreds of Thorne residents lining North Eastern Road to witness the end of an era.'

View from King Street looking westwards into The Green, with Orchard Street off-centre to the left. Around the time of the picture The Green contained an antique furniture dealer, a pork butcher, baker and a grocer.

View along Finkle Street, with the entrance to the Red Lion public house on the extreme left. Before closure in the 1960s, the premises could be traced back to at least 1723. Former owners included William Darley Ltd. According to the *Doncaster Gazette* of 1 May 1969: 'The Churchwardens and Overseers of the Poor realised [the pub's] attraction and convenient situation and in 1723 began to use it for their Vestry meetings...The Long Room along the frontage of the inn became their home – and in 1817 they resolved to buy it. The transaction was not finally made until 1819 when the deed of covenant was signed in Wakefield and Darleys [the pub's owners] were paid £300...The County Court Judge began to use the Long Room when he visited Thorne on his circuit. The magistrates too began to hold their court there.' The premises of Dickinson Bros, painters, are on the right.

North Eastern Road with a mill at the centre, whose occupants have included the Priestleys, the Gravils and the Oates.

The Blackamoor's Head public house on Church Street. It was also noted as the Black Head and as the Blackaboy's Head. The pub dates from at least 1822 and closed in 1906. Before closure, it was for a time tied to Darley's. At the time of the picture William Woodcock was the licensee.

View along Church Street. In addition to the Blackamoor's Head, situated on this thoroughfare, there was the Greyhound, which also closed in 1906.

View along Stonegate, with the vicarage on the left; a late eighteenth-century, three-storey building with a pediment. Kelly (1908) mentions that the living is a vicarage, net yearly value £229 including 60 acres of glebe, lying partly at Hatfield with residence, in the gift of H.R. Coventry esq of Monkton Park, Chippenham, Wilts and held since 1883 by Revd Joseph Johnson Littlewood Theol…Abraham De La Pryme, son of Matthew De La Pryme, a Flemish refugee, was perpetual curate here (1701-1714) and made a large collection for a history of the place and neighbourhood, now among the Lansdowne MSS, in the British Museum.

Church Street captured by the Arjay photographic company. The old Blackamoor's Head public house can be seen on the right.

106

Stonegate looking towards the church. Cottages on both sides of the street have since been demolished. The vicarage (the three storeyed-property on the right) has been converted to a nursing home.

Finkle Street, Thorne, stretching between the Market Place and The Green. Among this thoroughfare's former traders were: Tom Chapman jnr, tailor; Dickinson Bros, painters; Tom Garrett, butcher; Anne Jane Holland, fancy repository and boot warehouse; William Henry Lister, postmaster; W.A. Gilbey, wine and spirits merchants; Trimmingham & Co., drapers; William Wagstaffe, greengrocer and bill poster.

The new Thorne Grammar School was opened by Princess Mary, Countess of Harewood on 26 September 1930. At the opening, she planted a tree near the main gate. The cost of the building was £30,000 and a further £5,000 was spent on furniture and equipment. The new school could accommodate 300 pupils, and the first headmaster there was J.E. Shipley Turner MA.

Two views of South Parade, looking towards St Nicholas's church. The area has also been known as Bridge Gate. Another place of worship, the Primitive Methodist Centenary church (built in 1907), may also be identified. The Memorial Park is now to the right. Kelly (1908) recorded: 'There are [in Thorne] Wesleyan Methodist and Primitive Methodist chapels and a meeting house for the Society of Friends.'

Dutch Row, Moorends, Thorne. This was purpose-built in 1898 for immigrant Dutch workers, some of whom are depicted outside. Thorne is noted for its long association with peat cutting, which takes place on the extensive, adjacent moorland. Many Thorne inhabitants have peat-cutting ancestors, and a small number of residents still work there today. This is one industry which has helped focus attention on Thorne as a distinctive, self-supporting community.

Thorne Moors and peat workers. During the late nineteenth century the peat trade underwent a transformation. Peat took on a new, commercial use as animal litter, particularly for horses, which were then employed in Britain in huge numbers. Traditionally, peat had been worked as a fuel, but was a long-term victim of coal; the old fuel trade was virtually extinct by the early 1880s.

FIGHTING THE FIRE ON THORNE MOORS E

Fighting a fire on Thorne Moors. A number of companies exploited the Thorne peat as animal litter, each leasing a part of the moorland. Those companies surviving in 1896 merged their interests to form the British Moss Litter Co. A new 'British Moss' company was created in 1899, which survived until it was taken over by Fisons in 1963.

Peat worker. The immigration of Dutch workers to Thorne initially involved only a few, but it eventually numbered 300 people as families travelled across the North Sea to join their menfolk. All Dutch movement was eventually halted by the First World War and by the end of the war, the colony had greatly reduced in size. The Dutch, however, had made a distinctive contribution to the area, not only with their culture, but also with the peat winning methods they had introduced.

The four pictures here show scenes from Thorne's peace celebrations held on 18 July 1919. The *Doncaster Chronicle* of 25 July 1919 reported that the celebrations committee had arranged an excellent programme and, notwithstanding the short time for preparation, everything passed off in delightful fashion. Servicemen, ex-servicemen and civilian alike vied with each other, and throughout, the proceedings were marked with good-will and enthusiasm. The collectors did a hustle, and close on £200 was subscribed in a couple of days.

During the celebrations the town was gaily decorated and prizes were given for the most effective decoration. The programme proper was commenced on Friday (18 July), when the ex-servicemen and their wives were entertained to a sumptuous tea in the Temperance Institute, some 600 attending. Later in the evening a smoking concert was held in the town hall, where there was a packed attendance. Saturday, it was reported, was the great day of the feast. South Parade was crowded at two o'clock, at which time the procession commenced, headed by the Town Brass Band, the marshall being Lt. C. Stephenson.

Decorated conveyances and fancy dress costumes were much in evidence throughout the proceedings. School children on drays, in wagons and on foot numbered well over a thousand, with contingents from Medge Hall and Black Bull taking part. The procession paused near the Market Place where *God Save the King* was sung. After the town had been toured, the children assembled in the Hall grounds (kindly lent for the occasion by Mr E. Shipley) where they were provided with tea, and where the various trade exhibits and fancy dress costumes were judged.

Thorne men who had won distinctions in the Army were presented with medals by J. Servant, as well as war certificates and a sum of money. The Military Medal had been awarded to Sgt Edward Todd, Corporals Wm Robinson and Allan Robinson (brothers), Walter France, Herbert Godfrey, Wm Horton, Tom Scholes and Wm Rixon. All the men were heartily cheered. The children's sports were held during Saturday evening when the attendance was very large and the sport much enjoyed. The committee were congratulated and a special word of praise was felt to be due to R. Clark (chairman) and J. Servant (secretary).

Ellison Street, stretching from Southend to the junction with Bridge Street and Silver Street. The view here is looking north, towards the town centre. The properties to be seen include Milton House (right) and Bailey house (off-centre to the left). Noted former occupants of the street are William Elius Lunn, farmer; Richard Mindham, shopkeeper; Charles Pattrick, joiner; P. Roberts jnr, butcher; Enoch Shipley, farmer.

View along King Street, extending from Church Street/Market Place to Fieldside. Out of view on the left is Brooke's school, and the Wesleyan Chapel (built in 1826), which was restored in 1898, and renovated in 1995.

King Street, looking towards Darley's brewery and the North Eastern Hotel.

The church of St Nicholas is a small building of stone and rubble, chiefly in the Late Decorated style, consisting of chapel with north and south chapels, nave with clerestory, aisle and an embattled western tower, with pinnacles, containing a clock and bells, three additional bells being hung in 1892. The church was restored in 1860, when an organ was placed in the north chapel. There were sittings for 450 people. The register dates from 1565. It is tempting to suggest that the dedication to St Nicholas was due to the importance of the river trade, Nicholas being the patron of seamen.

Aerial view of the town centre, most likely taken from St Nicholas' church tower, looking down Church Street, to the Market Place. Many of the properties in the foreground on the left have been demolished. In the distance, off-centre to the right, is the town hall, which opened in 1884 and was subsequently used as a meeting place, concert hall, dance hall and market hall.

Aerial view, showing the Market Place off-centre to the right, c. 1926. The road leading into the Market Place from the lower left is Silver Street, while Finkle Street and King Street extend beyond the area.

Two views of Fieldside, Thorne, looking towards the town centre and Darley's brewery. On the left in the top picture is Thorne police station. On the right is a group of cottages carrying a stone with the inscription: 'Mayflower Buildings 1906'. On the left in the bottom picture is the Carnegie Library. The building's foundation stone was laid by James Servant on 14 December 1905.

Street scene at Thorne.

King Edward Road, Thorne, facing Thorne colliery. The gable on the building on the right carries a stone with the inscription '1904'. Out of view on the left is a property now known as Bennfield House nursing home.

118

Thorne South Station was opened on the Manchester, Sheffield & Lincoln Railway in 1866. The station is still used today. John B. Platt in *Thorne's First Railway* (1991) tells us that Thorne once boasted five railway stations.

Thorne North Station, by local photographer Thos Brewins. The station was opened on the North Eastern Railway in 1869 and still survives today.

Exterior view of Travis's Charity School, once an elementary mixed school, on Church Lane/Street. The buildings, erected in 1863 and enlarged in 1895, are of red brick with stone dressings, in the perpendicular, from designs by Messrs Brundell & Arnold, architects of Doncaster. At one time the school could hold 254 children and was endowed with one third of Travis's Trust. The premises closed as an infant and junior school during the early 1970s, though it continued in use as an annexe to the Grammar School for a few years. From 1982, it has been the home of renowned local sculptor Byron Howard.

Interior view of Thorne Infants School.

The 1911 Coronation celebrations outside the White Hart. The *Doncaster Chronicle* of 30 June 1911, mentioned that the town had a gay and festive appearance, decorations of many kinds being displayed on all sides, from the small cottage upwards. In the morning, services were held at the parish church and Wesleyan chapel, which were well attended. Immediately after the church service a meeting of the committee was held in the town hall to greet John Chester Coulman JP, the donor to the town of a large field, for the provision of a recreation ground for the town. Coulman personally handed over the title deeds. After lunch a huge procession was formed in the Hall grounds, kindly made available for the occasion by F.D. Foster.

Walking the greasy pole at the at the watermen's sports, held during Fair Week, June 1908.

During the celebrations G.B. Foster of Thorne Hall made a most efficient marshal, and helped by the committee, the procession was assembled in order. Just after two o'clock, headed by the marshal, they started to leave the ground. Following the marshal was a huge banner, appropriately worded for the occasion and featuring photographs of the King and Queen. Behind this the Thorne Brass Band and police followed. Close support was given by the magistrates and the clerk, ministers of religion, professional gentlemen, members of the district and parish councils, guardians, education committees and officials and the master and pupils of the Grammar School.

Behind the procession came an array of cyclists in costume on decorated machines, which made a good show. Following were boys and girls of the town on foot, and infant children on drays and other conveyances, numbering twelve or fifteen hundred in total. It was an imposing sight. After the children came light decorated vehicles and others, and next came what was the most successful part of the procession – trade exhibits.

Church Street with Hallgarth's shop on the left. Also on Church Street at this time, around 1910, were James Clarke, tailor and Mrs Maria Woodcock, private boarding house owner.

The business premises of Eddell Motors.

5-22. Thorne Colliery. Copyright

Messrs Pease and Partners acquired the mineral rights at Thorne Moorends from a private syndicate. The syndicate had put down a bore hole by the Calyx system, which conclusively proved the existence of a 9ft bed of Barnsley coal at a depth of 916 yards. Sinking was commenced at Thorne in November, 1909, and the two shafts were carried through the running sand by the end of the following January, when the work was kept standing for six months for the erection of headgear necessary before sinking through the new red sandstone. Directly this water-bearing strata was pierced the difficulties of the sinkers commenced. These and other difficulties continued until 1919 when, according to the *Doncaster Chronicle* of 22 August 1924 real substantial progress was made. The war naturally interfered with and in fact completely held up the work associated with the pit. However, in September 1919 the colliery directors definitely decided to go forward with the sinking by means of the cementation process of M. Francois, the well known Belgian engineer, who was then living in Doncaster. Consequently, during August 1924 the Barnsley bed was reached at Thorne. There was great rejoicing and much jubilation in the small town, and a Union Jack waved proudly over No. 1 shaft at the colliery. However, troubles continued to plague the colliery and it was abandoned in 1956.

William Marsdin Darley, born in 1827, was the founder of the family brewing business at King Street, Thorne. Before this, the Whitfield family had operated a brewery on the site and, when it was acquired by William, the Thorne Brewery was a modest concern. The exact date that W.M. Darley began brewing beer is unknown, but it is generally thought to be around 1850. By the 1860s, the annual turnover was just short of £21,000. By 1879, Darley's held rented property and employed an agent in Hull. During the 1880s there was a trade expansion in both the East and West Ridings. A household property and land list reveals that most of the brewery's tied houses were in Thorne. In 1892, W.M. Darley died in Bath at the age of 65.

Following his father's death Charles William Darley took control. Under his leadership it was said the business went forward in leaps and bounds. By 1902 the reconstruction of the brewery had been accomplished and the skyline of King Street, with its brick tower and chimney, was established. Also around this time, Charles and one of his sons, Charles Francis, forged links with the Milnthorpe family who were maltsers in Barnby Dun. Manor Maltings was established in which C.W. Darley became a director, and later Chairman of the Board. Both of Charles' sons, C.F. and T.B. Darley, were given shares in the company. C.W. Darley died in 1926.

Following his brother's death in 1933, Thomas Bladworth Darley, who had gained a degree in chemistry at Oxford, became chairman of the brewery and malt business. Under Thomas's direction, the brewery reached its greatest size and influence, owning a tied estate of about 100 houses. In October 1978, Darley's was acquired by Vaux Breweries of Sunderland. Thomas Darley died in 1982 aged 91. Remarkably he was still visiting the brewery six days before his death.

In May 1986, Vaux announced that Darley's Brewery would be closed in September of that year. Since that time, the brewery chimney has been demolished and the site cleared for commercial use.

Brewing Room foreman Arthur Bell tests the quality of the fermenting beer.

On 12 April 1962, the *Doncaster Chronicle* carried the following details on Thorne Marine Ltd, pictured above: 'The growing outdoor hobby of messing about with boats has been given a big boost by the bold and imaginative enterprise of Thorne Marine. They have opened a boat centre on the south banks of the Sheffield and South Yorkshire canal at Thorne…The Thorne Marine Centre [which opened on Saturday 14 April 1962] has been purpose-built and is a spacious, airy modern building where you will find displayed a great many fascinating things. There are the very latest and exciting small cruisers, launches, dinghies, canoes, and especially craft suitable for trailing. Also a fine selection of outboard motors, a well stocked chandlery store, a range of smart and business like marine clothing, plus up-to-the-minute water skis and underwater swimming equipment…'

CW00660859

UXBRIDGE
From Old Photographs

K. R. PEARCE

AMBERLEY

First published by Alan Sutton Publishing Limited, 1997
This edition published 2009

Copyright © K. R. Pearce, 2009

Amberley Publishing
Cirencester Road, Chalford,
Stroud, Gloucestershire, GL6 8PE

www.amberleybooks.com

British Library Cataloguing in Publication Data.
A catalogue record for this book is available from the British Library.

ISBN 978-1-84868-390-7

Typesetting and origination by Amberley Publishing
Printed in Great Britain

Contents

Cross Street, Uxbridge, 1960. This is one of the most attractive corners of old Uxbridge. The site of the former Catherine Wheel public house remains, although the property has become an antiques shop. When one building in the centre was demolished in 1936, the local newspaper said that Cross Street looked like 'a ragged set of teeth, with one of the front ones pulled out'. Nevertheless, sufficient character remained for the demolition of the remainder in 1969 to provoke a public outcry.

Acknowledgements

Sincere thanks are due to the following, whose photographs are used in this book: Hilda Browne, Bill Buckledee, Derek Buttrum, Don Chaney, the Gazette, Alan Hall, Julian Jephcote, Lionel Kirby, John Laker, Philip Sherwood and Christine Welford. The author also greatly appreciates the help received from Lily Craddock, Dennis Gardner, Betty Kingston, Tom Morgan, Arthur Playfair, Brian Simpson, Sally Underwood and Syd Wilson, and from Barbara Townsend who prepared his manuscript for publication.

Introduction

During the closing decades of the twentieth century, Uxbridge has become an office centre, with companies such as Burger King, Lincoln National, the Allied Irish Bank and Rank Xerox making their headquarters in the town. The office blocks have risen in a bewildering variety of shapes, sizes and materials, and still more are planned. A significant factor in this change is the excellent communications, for Uxbridge is a mere five miles from Heathrow Airport, is close to the M4, M25 and M40 motorways, and is linked to the London Underground system.

At the same time, much of the town centre has been redeveloped, and it now includes the grand Civic Centre and a large enclosed shopping precinct. The conservation movement came too late to influence this redevelopment greatly, but now hangs on grimly to those parts of the town that have survived the upheaval.

This book chronicles the period from 1950 to 1970, just before the onset of those sweeping changes. People who return to Uxbridge after years of absence are now inclined to lose their way. Most of those who have spent a lifetime in the area have little liking for the new town and much prefer what they used to see. Here is a renewed glimpse of those former days, but – be warned – the overworked verb in our story is 'demolish', for this is a sad record of the Uxbridge that has vanished.

K.R. Pearce
Uxbridge, 1997

The town centre, *c.* 1950. It is Wednesday afternoon – early closing day – and all is quiet. Nevertheless, the policeman on point duty by the market house directs a vehicle into the High Street. Traffic lights were installed here in 1954 – the first in the district.

5

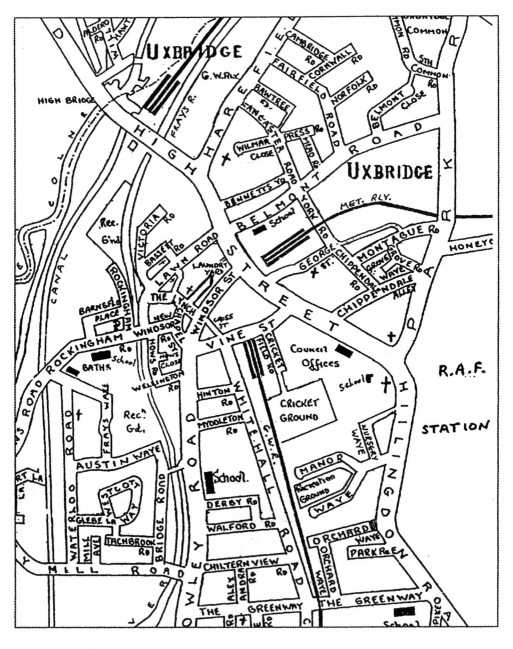

Street plan of Uxbridge, *c.* 1950.

SECTION ONE

FROM MARKET TOWN TO LONDON SUBURB

Early nineteenth-century print of Windsor Street, dominated by St Margaret's Church. This scene is still recognizable today.

Print of the town centre, 1818. Uxbridge emerged as a market town towards the end of the twelfth century and a market house was in existence by 1561. The market flourished in the later half of the eighteenth century, leading to the construction of a larger building in 1789. The new structure, which must then have dominated the main street, survives today as a symbol of the town's past.

The market house, 1971. The open ground floor has been enclosed to give protection to the stallholders, but this has spoiled the appearance of the building. More enlightened views have since prevailed. Market day in Uxbridge was Thursday, and still visible in the turret over the clock is the market bell. This was rung at noon each Thursday to mark the beginning of trading, and at 4.00 p.m. to bring proceedings to a close.

Cowley Mill on the River Frays, *c. 1925*. The flourishing corn trade inevitably brought business to the flour mills on the rivers Colne and Frays, and in the nineteenth century there were said to be ten mills in the vicinity of Uxbridge. One of these was Cowley Mill, also known at different periods as Rabb's Mill, Austin's Mill and Dobell's Mill. A fire in 1928 brought milling here to an end, but part of the building survives in the Hale Hamilton valve works.

Denham village, *c. 1900*. For centuries Uxbridge was the market centre for west Middlesex and south Buckinghamshire, and therefore the nucleus of a rural area. In the countryside round about were villages, such as Denham, that were farming communities. Here were the homes of the agricultural labourers and the yeomen. The construction of Denham film studios in the 1930s was destined to alter the character of the village dramatically

The nave and chancel of St Margaret's parish church, 1920s. Prominent in this view is the chancel screen, erected in memory of the fallen of the First World War. In 1922 T.E. Lawrence enlisted at RAF Uxbridge, under the assumed name of John Hume Ross, and was soon to be marched here for compulsory church parade – complete with bodkin-stick and bayonet. 'Bayonets are essential for divine service,' he commented wryly in his memoirs.

The old burial ground, Uxbridge, 1966. For several centuries St Margaret's Church was a chapel-of-ease of Hillingdon and it only acquired parish status in 1842. Uxbridge burials therefore took place at Hillingdon, until in 1576 the townsfolk were given this piece of land by the then lord of the manor, the Earl of Derby. Since its closure in 1855 the former cemetery has become a pleasant garden. In the background are the attractive old houses of Cross Street.

The High Street, *c.* 1905. In the early part of the twentieth century the character of Uxbridge began to change, and 1904 proved particularly significant. In that year the electric cars of the London United Tramways and the trains of the Metropolitan Railway both reached the town, thereby heralding the westward sprawl of London and the development of what has become known as Metroland. In this view two open-topped trams are in the section of the main street between Vine Street and Windsor Street.

The High Street, 1920s. Already the 'country town' atmosphere is beginning to fade, and Uxbridge is taking on the appearance of a suburban town. In the background a tram stands at the terminus, near the junction with Harefield Road. On the right, by Barclays Bank, is the narrow entrance into Belmont Road.

The town centre, 1933. The market house is on the left. The sophistication continues: shops that were once owned and run by local families are passing into the hands of chain stores. In this view you can see Lipton's, Eastman's dyers and cleaners, the Midland Bank, Boots the chemist and Mac fisheries. In 1937 most of the shops on the right were demolished to make way for the forecourt of the new underground station.

Cottages in Nash's Yard just prior to demolition. Uxbridge expanded rapidly in the early part of the nineteenth century – the age of the successful corn market and the stagecoach. Rows of cottages were then built in the yards and alleys off the High Street. A century later most were dilapidated and insanitary, and the Uxbridge Urban District Council embarked on a slum clearance scheme. These cottages were condemned in October 1932.

Hillingdon Village, 1930. Traffic was by now increasing on the London to Oxford road through Uxbridge, and Western Avenue was under construction to ease the congestion. Road-widening schemes were also being undertaken along the old highway. About four years later the shops and cottages on the left were cleared.

Hillingdon Hill, 1934. At the same time as the village street was widened, a dual carriageway was created on the western approaches. The old road (left) was destined to become the 'down' route. A steamroller is at work on the new upward side of the hill. The contractor for Middlesex County Council was G. Percy Trentham.

Clearing bomb damage, Montague Road, 1940. More of the old town disappeared in the Blitz, with this incident being one of the most serious. In the early afternoon of Sunday 6 October a string of bombs fell across north Uxbridge. A number of houses were either destroyed or badly damaged and ten people were killed.

Doodle-bug damage, The Greenway, 1944. At about 7.10 a.m. on 22 June, a VI rocket landed at the western end of The Greenway. Damage to buildings included 4 houses that were completely destroyed, 46 that were temporarily uninhabitable and 75 that needed extensive repair. Of the casualties, 7 people were killed, 25 were injured and taken to hospital and another 50 were treated on the spot for minor injuries.

SECTION TWO
THE STREET SCENE

The Lynch, from Rockingham Parade, 1963. The River Frays is in the foreground. In this context the word 'lynch' means slope or inclination – no one was ever lynched here!

Part of the High Street, late 1950s. On the left is the George Inn, one of the old coaching inns of Uxbridge. It was largely rebuilt in the 1930s. Woolworths and Suter's (later Owen Owen) survive today, but the buildings in the foreground were demolished for redevelopment in 1971. The line of vehicles indicates the growing problem of traffic congestion in the town centre.

The junction of the High Street with Harefield Road, 1965. On the right is 118 High Street, the offices of E.J. Garner & Co., solicitors. Next to the end of this building is Warwick Place, leading to the warehouses of Kirby Bros Ltd, builders' merchants. On the left is the southern end of Harefield Road. The raised footpath on the right leads past The Gables – a house occupied for many years by Dr W.A. Hotson, a local GP.

Northern end of Cowley Road, 1969, Mahjack's DIY store and the southern end of Windsor Street are in the distance. On the extreme left is the entrance to the yard of E. Plested & Son, a firm established in 1873 as carriage builders and wheelwrights, which inevitably switched to the motor trade. In the centre are the shops of Staniford the newsagent, Keyworth the baker and Staniford the draper.

Southern end of Vine Street, May 1969. In the centre are the Keyworth and Staniford shops shown above. On the left is The Wellington public house. On the right the mighty horse chestnuts in the old burial ground are in bloom.

Part of the High Street showing the narrow entrance to Lawn Road, 1968. No. 49 High Street (left) is empty, having been vacated the previous year by the grocery chain David Greig. On the right are the premises of H.C. Pearson the gents' tailor and outfitter, and Gregory's Garage, which is advertising the new Vauxhall Viva motor car.

Lawn Road from the High Street, 1966. The tall building in the centre was originally a private house called The Lawn, but in the 1860s the drive was opened up to the left of the building and extended southwards to the River Frays. The new thoroughfare was called Lawn Road, and houses were built on either side of it.

Buildings at the northern end of Lawn Road. Part of the white wall of Barclays Bank in the High Street is visible on the left. On the right are the shoe repair premises of George Webb, and beyond them the workshop of undertaker Percy Walding. His assistant, Leslie Miller, made coffins here for years.

Lawn Road, 1966. The Lawn, now a furniture and crockery depository for Randall's Stores, had clearly seen better days. The front gable of the Roman Catholic presbytery and the entrance to Osborn Road are on the left. On the right are some of the storage buildings of E.E. Chaney & Sons Ltd, dealers in corn and animal foodstuffs.

Lawn Road, further down towards the River Frays, 1964. On the extreme right is the front hedge of Lawn Road Methodist Chapel and the entrance to Cross Road, a short and narrow roadway leading to The Lynch. Some of the houses on the left still stand, but everything else has gone.

Bassett Road, 1968. This road was named after Gilbert Bassett, who was lord of the manor when a market was established in Uxbridge in the twelfth century. The 1950s telephone exchange looms on the left, and the Roman Catholic Church of Our Lady of Lourdes and St Michael is on the right. Between them you can glimpse a few of the houses in Osborn Road. The town centre relief road sliced through here in 1969, and today only four houses in a truncated Bassett Road survive.

SECTION THREE

THE SHOPS

The newsagents of Edwin R. Wescott, 124 High Street, 1968. This shop was soon to close. Wescott set up business here in 1904, and it was run latterly by his granddaughter, Jean Hobson, and her husband, Alan.

Windsor Street, 1966, shortly before the post office counter trade had been transferred to premises in Bakers Road. Fewer people needed to come to this street, which was a blow to the traders. Today, Windsor Street is a vital part of the Old Uxbridge conservation area.

Windsor Street shops, 1966. On the left, the grocery store of R. Simmonds (formerly Edwards & Simmonds) may have been small, but it had a reputation for the excellence of its cooked meats. In the distance is part of a terrace of houses in Chapel Street called Providence Row.

Nos 24-26 Windsor Street from The Lynch, October 1968. At No. 24, now selling tackle for anglers, Miss Hannah Baldwin had for many years run a toy shop – a treasure-house for children. Her brother Albert had been the gents' hairdresser next-door. The betting office of W. Hobbs & Co. reflects the permissive legislation of the 1960s. All of these properties were demolished, along with Cross Street, in December 1969. Langston's the ironmongers is just visible on the right.

Pearce the fishmonger, 46 Windsor Street, April 1970. Cecil and Lucy Pearce ran this business, which was established *c.* 1855 by Cecil's grandfather. Their handwritten advertisements, fish models and decorative shells all added character to the display. Cecil retired shortly after and the business closed.

H. Peddle's hardware store, 47 Windsor Street. This family business also dated back to the 1850s, and part of the attraction of the shop was the haphazard arrangement of goods on display.

Kate Peddle, aged 73, inside the hardware store, 1971. Soon after this photograph was taken she retired and the shop that was established by her grandfather was closed. Kate could produce anything – a flue brush, a fly swat, a mousetrap – despite the apparent confusion. The 'shoppers' table' on the wall is a reminder of the decimalization of currency that occurred that year.

Webb's boot and shoe repair shop, 48 Windsor Street, 1970s. This shop was next to the police station and was owned by Reg and Maud Watts. Here, Maud is at the shop door with her employee Fred Malpass, who carried out the repairs in a tiny workshop at the rear. In the early twentieth century this was a fish and chip shop run by Henry and Fanny Beach. You could get a good meal for a penny if you asked for a 'ha'p'orth and a ha'p'orth'.

Fred Malpass at the counter of the shoe repair shop. The shop was packed with items relating to the shoe and leather trade, and had been run by the same family since 1912.

Classic Georgian shop front of Rayner's the chemists, 39 High Street, 1970. This was an old-style shop, with carboys containing coloured liquid in the window. Inside were rows of labelled wooden drawers, and above the shelves were pestles and mortars as a reminder of the days of 'homemade' medicines. Shelves labelled 'horse and cattle medicines' latterly held deodorants for humans. The business was founded by Matthew Rayner in the early nineteenth century and remained in the family for four generations. The shop closed in 1962, when the last proprietor, Winifred Flowerdew, retired. The shop front was saved by the Museum of London and it remains in one of their stores to this day.

Nos 7 and 8 High Street, 1969. These shops were built in 1894, after a fire had severely damaged earlier buildings on the site. Leonard Saich, a member of a well-known Ickenham family, took over No. 7 as a gents' outfitters in 1930, when a sports jacket cost 8s 11d. At No. 8 the Home and Colonial grocery firm took over the shop from new, and were therefore one of the first chain stores to arrive in Uxbridge.

Sherwin's Dairy, 127 High Street, 1971. George Sherwin started this business in 1887 and kept his cows in a field off Harefield Road. The shop was at one time noted for its homemade ice cream. Sherwin died in 1939, and his daughter Nellie took over the dairy trade for a further four years. She then ran the business as a grocery shop.

Nellie Sherwin (right) and her assistant Florrie Dawson inside the grocery shop. The marble-topped table and counter, and the milk-bottle-shaped lampshade, are reminders of the former dairy trade. Behind Nellie is the door leading down to her cellar – the only form of refrigeration she had. The chair at the counter was for customers who wanted to sit down and chat. Through the window you can see the frontage of the newly opened Tesco supermarket. The competition was too much and Nellie was forced to close down.

The butcher's shop of R. Bonny & Son, 16b Cowley Road, 1970. The shop was started by Reg Bonny in the 1920s and was continued by his son Arthur. In the Uxbridge Directory the firm's advertisement emphasized 'orders delivered'. Sure enough, there is the delivery bicycle parked across the front door to the flat above the shop.

Arthur Bonny (right) and his assistant Fred Gilbert behind the counter of the butcher's shop. Mrs May Bonny was usually at the cash desk, which bore an advertisement for Bonny's 'Camberwell' pork sausages. Hubert was the delivery boy. There was fresh sawdust on the floor, and a friendly and personal service.

Nos 268-273 High Street, *c.* 1970. At No. 268 (left) was the shop of Perry & Routleff printers and stationers. At No. 269 was the butcher's shop of W.S. Gray & Son. At No. 270 was the draper's and outfitter's shop of J.W. Sigston. Everyone in Uxbridge knew this as the 'in-and-out shop', because for years it had no proper shop front. Once the roller blind was up you just walked in one side to view the goods and then came out the other. On the right is No. 273, previously occupied by dentists called Lakeman and Barr but now the office of the South of England Building Society.

Nos 207-210 High Street, 1961. From left to right are Bishop & Marsh estate agents, the Pillar Box Café, the bookshop of Tommy Barnard and the tailor's shop of F.W. Bowditch. In 1967 these buildings were demolished for redevelopment and Mr Barnard moved to a shop at 11 Windsor Street. He closed the business in 1996.

Nos 188-190 High Street, 1961. These shops were Milletts the outfitters, the Candy Shop for sweets and tobacco and Scannell's the greengrocers. The buildings were situated between George Street (left) and Bonsey's Yard (right) and they were of medieval timber-framed structure. In 1973 they were placed on a list of buildings of historical and architectural interest, but even before the list was published a development company bulldozed the lot out of existence.

The general shop of R. Ling, 107 The Greenway, April 1965. The shop was closed shortly after. It was incorporated into a house with a large garden, and the fruit trees on either side of the shop front gave a distinctive bygone and rural feel to the premises. The site was subsequently acquired by the borough council and the homes of Cornfield Close were built there.

Part of the High Street, 1966. Barclays Bank and the entrance to Belmont Road are on the left. Next are the Southern Electricity Board showroom, Vernon Brown ('everything for the farm and garden'), the George Inn (closed) and Maxwell's the tailors (also closed). These last four buildings were demolished, in 1971 for development, and this section of the street was later pedestrianized.

The next part of the High Street, 1970. The George Inn remains unoccupied and boarded up, but the shop next-door has become Farr Bedford estate agents. The hardware, wallpaper and paint departments of Kirby Bros Ltd are at 153 and 154 High Street, and the entrance to Cocks' Yard is on the right. All of these premises were demolished in 1971.

Kirby Bros tool department, 57 and 58 High Street. The tool department was housed here from 1951 to 1966. For many years prior to this, these premises had been Hall's china shop. By 1966 a major town centre redevelopment scheme had been prepared and the demolition of the premises was forecast. Clearance began in 1968.

Part of the High Street. Although the buildings on the right survived the 1968 demolition, the others did not. They were (left to right) Miles Motors, Sewmaster sewing machines, Cave House Yard, The Louvre ladies' fashions and Joshua Baker, Cooke and Standen estate agents. The Tesco supermarket was eventually to occupy this site.

Nos 53-56 High Street. These shops also disappeared in 1968. They were (left to right) Gregory's Garage (with Cleveland Petrol sold across the pavement), W. & F. Eves estate agents, N. Osborne Fardon opticians, Molly Travers children's clothes and Dr Scholl's foot comfort service. Above the last of these were the offices of Pinkney, Keith Gibbs & Co., chartered accountants.

The premises of David Greig, the grocery chain, 49 High Street, just before the shop closed in April 1966. On the right you can just glimpse Lawn Road. David Greig came to Uxbridge in 1904 and had an agreement with Sainsbury's that they would never compete with each other in the same town, but Sainsbury's eventually arrived in Uxbridge in 1978.

The butcher's shop of Joseph Nicholls, New Windsor Street, 1966. This family business opened in the High Street *c.* 1830 and moved to New Windsor Street about fifteen years later. It was recognized that Nicholls' pork sausages were the best for miles around. This was probably the last shop in the town where wooden shutters were put over the windows each evening at closing time. Joseph Nicholls died in 1968 and the building was demolished the following year.

The wallpaper shop of Nickolay Ltd, Cross Street, 1963. The building on the left is clearly of timber-framed construction and shows evidence of pargetting. The tall building has large sash windows and a decorative iron balcony. This mixture of styles was part of the appeal of Cross Street.

Nos 137-140 High Street, 1954. Mulhollands shoe shop, part of the Norvic chain, was rebuilt in 1936. Next-door is Chaney's bakery shop, which was established there in 1865 by Joseph Truss Chaney. A new shop front was installed there in 1933. Chaney's was run by the family for four generations, but the bakery business closed in 1954. The narrow entrance to Bennett's Yard separates this shop from the Uxbridge branch of Barclays Bank.

The first stage of the building of a new shopping precinct is underway, as evidenced by the cranes in the background, August 1969. All of the shops beyond the market house await demolition. Prominent in this scene is the store of Montague Burton ('the tailor of taste'), which opened in February 1938. Above the shop was Burton's Dance Hall, a popular venue for young people in the post-war period. The Inland Revenue also had an office in this building.

SECTION FOUR

PUBLIC HOUSES

Gas holders in Cowley Mill Road overwhelm the Black Prince beerhouse. This inn was run for more than forty years by the Guest family It closed its doors in January 1969.

The Chequers Hotel, 40 High Street, 1960. The hotel closed shortly after. This was one of the great coaching inns of Uxbridge, where horses were changed on the first 'stage' out of London. The archway led to an extensive yard, which at one time housed a market for cattle, sheep and pigs. The buildings were demolished after trading ceased and for a short time the site was used as an open market.

The Kings Arms, 19 High Street. This inn also harks back to the days of the stagecoach. It also closed in 1960, and was used briefly as a restaurant and then a garden centre. More recent alterations have ruined the appearance of the ground-floor frontage. The first local newspaper, the *Middlesex and Buckinghamshire Advertiser*, was printed in 1860 from an office in the yard of the Kings Arms (left).

The Falcon public house, 120 High Street, 1966. This inn actually began as a beerhouse next-door at No. 119. The move took place in 1924, and the former premises (with the white-painted frontage) then became the Fairy Belle restaurant. No. 120 had previously been a pair of semi-detached town houses, which was still evident at this time. Perhaps as a gesture to our links with Europe, the Falcon was renamed the Continental in 1984.

The Eight Bells public house. The demolition of this inn in 1972 saddened many local people, but its remains lie underneath the St Andrew's roundabout today. In his 1922 memoirs *The Mint*, T.E. Lawrence, then masquerading as aircraftsman John Hume Ross, mistakenly called it the Seven Bells. Since the pub was so close to St Andrew's Church, people often assumed that the eight bells were in St Andrew's tower, but in fact the inn pre-dates that church and was named after the (then) eight bells of St John's Church, Hillingdon.

The Railway Arms, Vine Street, 1962. This inn dates back to the coming of the Great Western Railway to Uxbridge in 1856, although an earlier beerhouse on the site was called The Swan. In 1976 it was renamed The Printer's Devil, because of its patronage by workers at the nearby King & Hutchings printworks. Closure and demolition came in 1980.

The Carpenters Arms beerhouse, Vine Street. This public house closed its doors for the last time in 1954, but the building was not demolished until 1976. In the 1960s it was used temporarily as a canteen by King & Hutchings employees while their premises were being rebuilt. In the yard on the right are cottages in Janes Place.

The Wellington public house, No. 35 Vine Street, 1969. Named after the great Duke of Wellington, this inn is believed to have opened in 1830 when he was Prime Minister. It was demolished *c*. 1970 and was replaced by an office block called Wellington House. (See also p. 17.)

The Walmsley Arms, Harefield Road, 1960. In 1939 this public house was threatened with closure, because the Abrook Arms had been extensively rebuilt almost next-door. Nevertheless it survived until November 1961, after which the site became a car park for the Abrook Arms.

The Black Horse public house, 43 Waterloo Road, 1962. This inn closed *c.* 1966 and the site was later redeveloped, but the acute observer can still find a sign saying Black Horse Yard in Waterloo Road.

The Van and Horses, Cowley Road, May 1969. On the right is the iron footbridge over the River Frays, which leads to Bridge Road and Austin Way. The 'improvement' of Cowley Road led to the clearance of the property in October 1972. The former Cowley Road is now a service road in front of Whitehall School.

SECTION FIVE
TRANSPORT

Cowley station on the West Drayton–Uxbridge branch line of the Great Western Railway, 1950.

Jim Stone and three Uxbridge Council dray horses, Waterloo Road stables, 1950. At that time the decision had been made for two of the horses to retire to a farm on the Isle of Wight, but Captain (centre) stayed on. For Jim, who lived in Bennetts Yard, it was a seven-day week, but he did it gladly. Both Jim and Captain retired in March 1953. Horsedrawn traffic was rapidly beginning to disappear from the streets.

An Uxbridge-bound train waiting in the cutting near the Greenway Bridge for the signal to change, August 1958. This 'push-and-pull' train consisted of the 0-4-2 tank engine and one carriage. In the background is one of the hedges bordering the Lowe and Shawyer cut-flower nursery.

Diesel railcar W30 pausing at Cowley station on its way to West Drayton, August 1960. These former GWR railcars were used on the branch from the mid-1950s. In the distance is the bridge carrying Peachey Lane over the rails. This station, opened in 1905, was closed in 1962. Three years later nearly every trace of the station was removed.

Interior of Vine Street station, August 1962. One optimistic traveller is awaiting the next train. The 'perishables' van (right) was brought in by the first train each morning, remained at the platform for the rest of the day, and left for Paddington on one of the last through trains. It is said that W. S. Gilbert, while waiting for a train here in the 1880s, saw a poster advertising the Tower of London, and that this inspired him to write *The Yeomen of the Guard*.

A single-car British Rail diesel unit approaching the Greenway Bridge from Uxbridge, August 1962. There was a steep 1 in 64 gradient here as the train from the terminus entered the cutting alongside Cleveland Road. The Cowley Brick public house is at the end of Chiltern View Road (top left).

Two little girls on the platform of the Vine Street terminus, 9 September 1962. The passenger service on the branch line was to be withdrawn the following day, so the father of these girls ensured that their last journey to West Drayton and back was recorded. Freight traffic on the line ceased in February 1964, and when parcels traffic ended in July of that year the station closed.

Vine Street station signal-box. This box was shut down on 18 October 1962, and some wag has chalked 'For Sale 2/6' on the wall. On the right are the houses at the east end of Myddleton Road. The signal-box was built in 1920 and was of standard Great Western Railway design.

Vine Street frontage to the station, July 1965. Demolition is already beginning in the background. On either wing of this building there were shops. On the right is the former coal office of Rickett, Smith & Cockerell. On the left were the Burr & Gibbons coal office and the Maison Lucena ladies' hairdressers.

Demolition of Vine Street station, July 1965. On the left is the canopy roof of the platform lying at an angle, having been cut off near ground level. The station was opened by the Great Western Railway in 1856, back in the days of their broad-gauge trains. Today some of the platform edges can still be detected, for the site is now an NCP car park.

Uxbridge High Street station, 1955. The Great Western Railway opened a second branch to Uxbridge in 1907, this one southwards from Denham. The line was never a commercial success, and the outbreak of the Second World War in 1939 gave the company a good excuse for closing the passenger service. It was never restarted. Shortly after this the remains of the station were cleared away.

Freight yard, Uxbridge High Street station, 1963. Although the passenger service had ceased, goods traffic continued here, including coal for Charringtons Ltd, which had an office in the station buildings. The building of a modern coal depot at West Drayton was a major factor in the complete closure of both former Great Western Railway branch lines in 1964.

Goods yard, Uxbridge High Street Station, December 1963. By now traffic was restricted to one early morning train each day, using a locomotive based at the Southall shed. In January 1964 the line was closed. The Braybourne Close housing development now occupies this site.

Showrooms of Norman Reeves Ltd, 215-219 High Street. The period covered by this book (1950-1970) was a time when car ownership increased rapidly. It was a good era, therefore, for car dealers. Reeves was one of the largest in the district. The showrooms and extensive workshops could also be reached from George Street. The firm was founded in the 1920s by Norman Reeves, who was a native of Margate.

The original Belmont Road station, the terminus of the Metropolitan and Piccadilly lines, July 1965. Opened in 1904 when the underground system first reached Uxbridge, this station had become inadequate by the 1930s. The present terminus was ready in December 1938, and this old station was then sold to the wholesale grocery firm of Alfred Button & Sons and incorporated into its adjacent premises. A Sainsbury's supermarket now occupies the site.

London Transport trains standing in the York Road sidings, October 1960. These particular carriages, known as 'F' stock, were notable for their oval-shaped windows at either end and their tendency to rock violently at speed. They were withdrawn in 1962.

Part of the London Transport sidings in Uxbridge, taken from Montague Passage, August 1967. The locomotive is an ex-Great Western Railway pannier tank, repainted in London Transport livery. There was still considerable goods traffic on the line at this time, but it soon declined. Today most of the former goods sidings have been converted into car parks for commuters.

Red 222 bus bound for Hounslow Central station waiting at the terminus in Bakers Road, March 1961. The building of the new underground station was combined with the opening up of Bakers Road in 1938 as a bus station. The presence of the Norwich Union building and Colham House behind the bus show that Bakers Road was rapidly being lined with offices and shops.

Bakers Road bus terminus from the York Road end looking towards the station and Suter's store, c. 1970. The tower of St Margaret's Church is at the top left and the London Transport staff canteen is centre right. The site in the foreground was later redeveloped, and a new bus garage, which was part of the scheme, was ready in 1983.

The original bus garage on the Oxford Road, Denham, 1981. Bus services began in the Uxbridge area in 1921, and in the following year this garage was opened by the London General Omnibus Co., which was then running local routes. The garage was doubled in capacity in 1954 by the construction of another building on the west side. The whole complex closed in 1983 and an office block named River Court now occupies the site.

Trolley buses at the Uxbridge terminus at the western end of the High Street, September 1959. The 607 trolley-bus route was inaugurated on 16 November 1936 and ran from Shepherds Bush to Uxbridge. Before that, electric trams had covered the route. The vehicles were based at the Hanwell depot. They moved smoothly along the roads and had rapid acceleration.

A 607 trolley bus, having just left the Uxbridge terminus, climbs the bill past the Odeon cinema, 1960. This particular vehicle, Q1 type No. 1768, survives today in the London Transport Museum collection. In the distance you can just distinguish the canal bridge near the Swan and Bottle public house. Since the building of the town centre relief road in 1971, this section of the High Street has become a cul-de-sac.

Pupils from Bishopshalt School queue to board a trolley bus outside the Red Lion, September 1960. Headgear as part of their school uniform was still *de rigueur*, but later in the decade the obligation to wear hats or caps faded. The last 607 trolley bus ran on 9 November 1960.

Routemaster bus waiting at the Uxbridge terminus, early 1966. Routemaster buses took over from the trolley buses and route 607 was renumbered 207. Behind this bus is the Hillside Café (see also page 62), where most drivers and conductors spent their breaks. We get a further view of the Odeon cinema here, which was opened in 1938. On 19 March 1966 this terminus was closed, and the 207s used the Bakers Road bus station thereafter.

A 207 Routemaster bound for Shepherds Bush stops outside Uxbridge market house, November 1960. This is less than a month since the trolley buses were withdrawn, so the overhead wires and supporting poles are still in position. In the 1980s, sections of the High Street were pedestrianized, so buses then travelled along the town centre relief road.

SECTION SIX

BUILDINGS

Cottages and a small shop in The Lynch, 1967. This is a glimpse of the Uxbridge of Victorian times.

No. 57 Cowley Road, 1970. This ordinary end-of-terrace house may seem unremarkable, but already the trend to improve or modernize one's home was underway. Original period features were being replaced by new and, many would say, unsympathetic ones.

Dental surgery of Mr E.A. Barr, 273 High Street, 1961. The dignity of this town house is impressive. Steps lead to the imposing front door and the iron railings contain a gate (left) giving access to the cellar. Shortly afterwards a modern glossy shop front was installed on the ground floor.

Medieval timber-framed interior of H.R.S. Turner's antique shop, Cross Street, 1969. At this time, demolition was just beginning. For many years the property had been the Catherine Wheel public house, but it closed in 1926. These lovely old timbers were saved for re-use elsewhere.

Cowley Grove, Cowley Road, 1965. Once a fine house in a large estate, this was at one time the home of actor and theatre manager John Rich (1692-1761), the pioneer of pantomime in England. Latterly run as a hotel, the property was demolished in 1967.

Nos 3 and 4 Hillingdon Road, February 1968. These cottages stood next to Turnpike Lane, and were built in the days when the Uxbridge turnpike gate or tollgate was across the road here. The cottages were condemned in the 1960s and were eventually replaced by the Concorde Close development.

Nos 27-31 Hillingdon Road. These fine nineteenth-century houses had been the homes of people who could afford to live in some style – with a servant or two. In the post-war era those days were past, so the September Court development replaced them in 1971.

Uxbridge High Street, 1966. The Hillside Café is on the left (see also page 55). The Red House next-door, 113 High Street, was a sixteenth-century property much altered. Life in the house *c.* 1900 is vividly described in *Memoirs of a Veterinary Surgeon* (1952), the autobiography of Reginald Hancock. Demolition came in 1967.

Providence Row, Chapel Street, 1960, These terraced homes, built in 1795 at the same time as Providence Chapel, stood near the junction of Cowley Road, Windsor Street and Vine Street. The southern wall of the former burial ground is on the right. The construction of the relief road was the reason for the removal of these houses in May 1969.

The former Cowley Road Boys' School, May 1961. This school, run initially by the British Society, opened here in 1835. It was closed in 1929 and for the next decade the building was the home of Uxbridge Library. During the Second World War it became a canteen and rest centre for HM Forces, and also a school meals canteen. The Salvation Army (see p. 80) used it for a short time while its new citadel was being built at the rear of the premises. The building was demolished in 1974.

The former militia barracks in Villier Street, 1962. Built *c.* 1855 for the Royal Elthorne Light Infantry Militia, this development included two rows of cottages as married quarters named Enfield Place. The militia transferred to Hounslow in 1879, when the building was sold. Later uses included a mission hall for St Andrew's Church, the headquarters of Uxbridge Athletics Club, a museum about the poet Thomas Gray, a centre for Uxbridge Labour Party and a judo club. The area was cleared in 1967 for the Enfield Close housing scheme.

The Belmont Café and adjacent houses, Belmont Road, 1960. The café was originally the stable block of the White Horse public house; but it was converted into a café between the wars. It closed in 1964, and the removal of the building gave increased parking space for the pub. The houses beyond it faced Bakers Road. They were demolished in 1970 to make way for a row of shops.

Guildford Villas, 29 and 31 Cowley Road, *c.* 1970. This imposing pair of semi-detached homes was built *c.* 1865 by William Guildford, a High Street watchmaker. From 1871 to 1874 the *Punch* artist and illustrator E. Linley Sambourne (1844-1910) lived at no. 29 with his mother and aunt. The villas were demolished in 1977 to make way for the Cobden Close buildings.

Penclose, 12 Harefield Road, *c.* 1950. This house, built in 1838, became the home of the Sambourne family for a short time after they left Cowley Road. It ceased to be a family residence in 1939, and was thereafter used as office and storage accommodation. Kirby Bros Ltd, builders' merchants took it over in the late 1960s. It was demolished in 1990.

The farmhouse of Hillingdon House Farm, Honeycroft Hill, from the southern end of North Way July 1965. This had ceased to be a working farm earlier that year, when the last tenant was given notice to quit by the borough council. After use as a council depot and plant nursery for some time, the house and former farmyard were sold for housing.

The north side of Partridge Villas, 1967. This cul-de-sac off Cricketfield Road, built in 1885, consisted of sixteen houses and ended abruptly at the sidings of Vine Street station. In January 1968 a disastrous fire destroyed much of the adjacent King & Hutchings printworks. This led to the redevelopment of the area in 1973, the clearance of Partridge Villas and the erection of the Boundary House office block.

Prospect Terrace, 4-14 Cowley Road, April 1968. On the left are some of the trees in the old burial ground. At the far end of this terrace lived one of Uxbridge's most valued tradesmen – Mr Wilson the chimney-sweep. He was sometimes engaged to appear at weddings in a suitably blackened condition, since it was thought that the presence of a sweep would bring good luck to the couple.

Chiltern View Terrace, 178-186 Cowley Road, 1966. The Chiltern View Tavern is on the right and the River Frays is in the foreground. The front doors of these houses were several feet above pavement level, and access was obtained from a central entrance with a flight of steps on either side. The terrace was made the subject of a clearance order in August 1966 and was later demolished.

No. 264 High Street, 1973. This was one of a pair of fine Victorian town houses, which were acquired by Uxbridge Council between the wars and converted into council offices. The treasurer's department was based at No. 264 in the post-war period. The building of Hillingdon's civic centre necessitated their destruction.

Offices of Fassnidge, Son & Norris Ltd, building contractors, 267 High Street. One is tempted to think that this Victorian building was constructed from components left over from the firm's numerous contracts – including St Andrew's Church. The company left the building in 1962. It was then used as council offices until its demolition in 1975.

Denham Lodge, *c.* 1950. This house, just over the county boundary in Buckinghamshire, was built by a flour miller named Henry Mercer in the 1870s. Between the wars it housed a preparatory school for boys, and after the Second World War it became a hotel. Demolished in September 1963, it was immediately replaced by the present Denham Lodge block of apartments.

Elmfield, Fairfield Road. This house was built in 1870 by the High Street chemist John Charles Rayner. During the Second World War it was taken by the Uxbridge division of the British Red Cross, and after the war remained as the Red Cross headquarters and a residential home for the elderly. A row of mock Georgian houses replaced it *c.* 1970.

The rear of Old Bank House, 64 High Street, 1968. This eighteenth-century house was originally a private bank, but it was converted to a family residence *c.* 1860. In 1937 it became the offices of Turberville Smith & Co., solicitors. By 1968 it had become council offices. The garden at the rear at one time stretched down to the River Frays.

The former Middlesex County Council offices off the High Street, 1970. Built in the late 1930s, these premises included a library and health clinic, as well as administrative offices. The creation of the London borough of Hillingdon in 1965 led to the need for a civic centre in the 1970s, and much of this building is now incorporated into that structure. Even the rooftop turret has been re-used.

Uxbridge Waterworks, Waterloo Road, 1967. This building was erected in 1864 by the Local Board of Health in an attempt to provide a continuous supply of fresh water for the whole town, but that was not achieved until the completion of the water tower near Uxbridge Common in 1907. The lowering of the water table in more recent times made the building redundant, and demolition in 1981 was followed by the erection of the Rushes Mead housing development.

Public baths, Waterloo Road, 1975. The baths opened in 1914, but even after the Second World War there were still hundreds of houses in Uxbridge without a bathroom. There were six cubicles in the bathhouse, and in the 1950s you could get a bath of hot water, a piece of soap and the use of a towel for 5d. The building closed in 1975.

Public conveniences. These two buildings in Windsor Street, wedged between the market house and St Margaret's Church, date from 1915. They were provided by the Uxbridge Urban District Council and were in use until 1929. Today they both still survive, the front one as a small shop.

Uxbridge Fire Station, Vine Street, 1963. This building opened in 1910 as the Electric Empire Cinema and was converted into a fire station by the Middlesex County Council in 1934. The fire brigade moved to its present headquarters in Uxbridge Road, Hillingdon, in 1964, when the building became a Youth Workshop. The 1984 demolition preceded the Charter Place development.

SECTION SEVEN
EDUCATION

St John's Church of England School, Uxbridge Moor. This school existed from 1843 to 1980, but the building survives as office accommodation.

The former St Margaret's School, The Lynch, 1963. This Church of England primary school for boys and girls, attached to St Margaret's Church, opened in 1865. Closure came in 1928, but the buildings remained for another forty-one years. During the Second World War they were used by the National Fire Service. They then housed a commercial firm in the post-war period.

The former Hillingdon and Cowley Boys' School. This was always called the Turnpike Lane School by local people. It too closed in 1928. The building remained, however, and was used for a time as a social club by the employees of the Lowe & Shawyer cut-flower nursery. Later, William Benford, the proprietor of a gaming machine company, used the building as a private club for his friends. Today, with two-storey extensions at each end, the old school has become offices.

Belmont Road Infants School, 1962. A charity school for girls, the Uxbridge School of Industry, opened here in 1816 and emphasized needlework and domestic skills. It became a county infants school in the 1928 reorganization of education in the Uxbridge area. In 1968 the school moved from this cramped accommodation and small tarmac playground (see below). The buildings were replaced in 1986 by the Allied Irish Bank development.

The site for the replacement school, 1962. In 1938 Middlesex County Council purchased this meadowland in Belmont Road, which was part of the grounds of a house called The Hermitage, The outbreak of war meant that the land was used for allotments and for an ARP wardens' post. It was not until the 1960s that pressure from north Uxbridge parents led to the building of the Hermitage School here. The school opened in the summer term of 1968.

One of the two Victorian buildings at St Andrew's Church of England School, 1970. This parish school, at one time for girls only, opened in 1869 and was enlarged in 1894. The construction of the St Andrew's roundabout required the demolition of these buildings, so the pupils moved to a new school on an adjacent site in 1972.

Park Lodge, Park Road, 1965. This building was demolished shortly after. Formerly a private house, it was the home of a local benefactor named John Chippendale in the early part of the nineteenth century (hence Chippendale Waye nearby). In 1931 Mrs Helen Bussell took over the house for her Uxbridge Business College, giving training in commercial subjects. Later, Park Lodge School, a private school for boys and girls, was run in the same building. There were seven teachers and ninety pupils when that school closed in 1960. Park Road day nursery is now on the site.

Senior pupils from Whitehall Junior School visiting the Houses of Parliament, *c.* 1955. Standing behind the children are Miss Dorothy Hillier (left), who taught at Whitehall from 1927 to 1966, and Miss Helen Jenkins, the headteacher. The gentleman on the left is Frank Beswick, Uxbridge's first Labour MP. He held the seat from 1945 to 1959, had a specialist knowledge of the aircraft industry and was later created a life peer.

The top class at Whitehall School make a presentation of a cine-camera to Miss Jenkins, the headteacher, in the playground, July 1968. The children were about to move on to secondary school. Miss Jenkins retired at the end of that year after thirteen years in the post. The other teacher is Mrs Sheila Collett, a former pupil.

Frays College, Harefield Road. This was a private school for boys and girls. It was founded by Capt. John Bennett and in 1928 moved to these premises, which had been a private house called Kent Lodge. A new classroom block (left) was added in the early 1930s. When headmaster Henry Stapley retired in 1974, the school closed and the building became Frays Adult Education Centre.

Uxbridge Technical College, 1968. Plans for a technical college in Uxbridge were laid in the 1930s, and this site off Park Road was set aside for the project. The land reverted to agricultural use in the war years, and it was a long time before the scheme was resurrected. The college eventually opened in 1965, and has expanded steadily ever since. The title was later changed to Uxbridge College.

SECTION EIGHT
THE CHURCHES

Lawn Road Methodist Chapel, 1960. Primitive Methodists built this church in 1876, and it had a small but devoted congregation. In 1957 it merged with the congregation at the Central Hall, and the Christian Science Society acquired the property. They ceased to hold services here in 1995, when the building became a day nursery.

The former Roman Catholic church, Lawn Road, 1962. This was the first Roman Catholic church in Uxbridge and was opened in 1892. This 'tin tabernacle' lasted until 1931, when it was replaced by the present church of Our Lady of Lourdes and St Michael a short distance away. The old building was bought by E.E. Chaney, the corn dealer, who used it as a store and added this single-storey office on the front.

The headquarters of the Uxbridge Corps of the Salvation Army, George Street, just before closure in 1971. The building opened as a Baptist Chapel in 1854, but the cause never prospered. Renamed Montague Hall in 1880, it was then hired out for public meetings. The Salvation Army moved here in 1898, and remained for 73 years.

Uxbridge Methodist Church, Park Road, in April 1972. Opened in 1930 as the Central Hall, it remained a place of worship until September 1972 when the congregation transferred to Christ Church. In this photograph the roof of the Regal cinema can be seen on the left, and Park Court flats on the right. The Uxbridge war memorial stood in the centre foreground, but had just been removed to the old cemetery in Windsor Street.

Interior of the Central Hall from the gallery, showing the rostrum, choir stalls and organ. There were seats for 750 people. Concerts and public meetings were also held here, for there was no other hall of comparable size in the town. Latterly there were problems with subsidence, so an office block was built on the site in 1985.

Old Meeting Congregational Church, Beasley's Yard, 1961. The building partly dates back to 1716, but the tower and frontage shown here were added in 1883. In 1962 the congregation from Providence Church (see p. 84) joined the Old Meeting members and the building was renamed Uxbridge Congregational Church. The opening of Christ Church in 1972 meant that the building was no longer required for worship, and it was renamed Watts Hall after Isaac Watts the hymn writer.

Interior of Old Meeting, 1961. The central pulpit indicates the heavy emphasis placed on preaching in Nonconformity. The William Hill organ was installed in 1905. The three memorial tablets on the far wall, to Revd Thomas Beasley, Mrs Phoebe Beasley and Revd William Walford, are now to be found on the wall of Beasley's Yard.

Tableau at the Sunday School Anniversary, Old Meeting, June 1953. Standing at the back towards the left is Horace Nash, the superintendent. The lady on the left wearing a dark suit and white blouse is Dorothy Bouch, the wife of the minister. The custom of sending your child to Sunday School, whether you attended church or not, was rapidly declining – television and the family car proved to be greater attractions.

Providence Congregational Church, The Lynch, 1966. This building dates from 1796, although the impressive frontage appeared nearly a century later. In the early twentieth century this was a flourishing church, but problems arose in the 1930s from which it never really recovered. The members merged with their fellow Congregationalists at Old Meeting in 1962, and seven years later the buildings were cleared away. Grainge's car park now stands on the site.

The last diaconate at Providence Church, 1960. Back row, left to right: R.H. Gurdler, J. Bodger, A.H. Randall (of Randall's Stores in Vine Street), J. Collett and D.F. Chatt (organist). Front row: Miss E. Brownie, R.J. Reeves (secretary), Revd G. Tegfryn Williams, H.S. Rooke and Miss D. Martin.

SECTION NINE
LEISURE & SPORT

The Odeon cinema, High Street, *c*. 1980. Opened in June 1938, this building was converted into three small cinemas in 1976. Closure in 1982 was followed by demolition, and a new Odeon appeared as part of an office development in 1990.

Interior of the Odeon, 1950. There were 622 seats in the gallery and 1215 in the stalls. Before television came along as a competitor, 'going to the pictures' was an immensely popular pastime, and queues frequently formed as patrons waited to enter the dark, smoke-laden chamber.

Female staff at the Odeon, c. 1950. The usherettes wore dark-green uniforms, with silver braid on lapels and sleeves, pill-box hats, pure silk and, rayon stockings, and silver high-heeled shoes that were painted each week to keep them shining. Before opening time they lined up military-style for inspection. Points were awarded for smartness, competence and courtesy, and could eventually merit a silver medal.

The Savoy cinema, at the junction of the High Street and Vine Street, 1960. This cinema opened in October 1921 on the site of the former town hall. It seated more than a thousand people. It closed in June 1960 and then for some years housed a bingo and social club. Redevelopment followed in 1983, and the Royal Bank of Scotland branch now occupies the site. The former Westminster Bank building (right) also disappeared in this project.

The impressive art deco interior of the Regal cinema. This cinema opened on Boxing Day 1931 and had seats for 1700 patrons. The detached console of the Compton organ is below the centre of the screen. Closure came in November 1977, but the building was Grade II listed. With its shell more or less intact, the former cinema survives today as the nightclub Discotheque Royale.

The former cinema at RAF Uxbridge, *c.* 1970. This was for many years the main entrance to the RAF station, but in 1972 it was blocked up and a new entrance was made about 50 yards to the south. The doors of this cinema first opened in May 1919, and from then until the outbreak of the Second World War it was open to the public. By then local people had a choice of four cinemas in the town, as well as others a few miles away in Yiewsley, Hayes and Ruislip.

A competitor in the driving marathon pauses between the fences in the main jumping arena at the Hillingdon Show, June 1966. The show can be traced back to humble beginnings, when the Uxbridge and District Horticultural Society held a one-day event in the grounds of Hillingdon Court, Vine Lane, in 1909. In the 1930s the Uxbridge Show, as it became known, began to attract large crowds. With the advent of the new borough in 1965 it was renamed the Hillingdon Show, and four years later became a two-day event. It is now known as the Middlesex County Show.

Pavilion at Uxbridge Cricket Club, August 1968. The first match at this ground, at the end of Cricketfield Road, took place in May 1858. Prior to this, matches were played on Uxbridge Common. Town centre redevelopment forced the club to move to its present venue off Park Road. The last game played here was in October 1970. Cricketfield Road has never been renamed.

Uxbridge Football Club ground, Honeycroft, Cleveland Road, March 1969. The club was formed in 1871, but for more than seventy years it had no permanent home ground. From 1923 it used the stadium pitch in RAF Uxbridge, and then in 1948 a small group of supporters formed a company to purchase the Honeycroft site. The club remained here until its move to Horton Road, Yiewsley, in 1978.

Honeycroft, the headquarters of Uxbridge Football Club, March 1964. This building was erected in 1891, and it remained a private house until 1947. It was then purchased on behalf of Uxbridge Football Club by local builder W.S. Try for £5,800. The club's manager was able to live in a flat on the premises. The houses of Ratcliffe Close occupy the site today.

A section of the crowd at Honeycroft, January 1960. At this time Uxbridge lost to Maidenhead United in the FA Amateur Cup. Second from left in the centre row is 'Jimmy' Jenkins, a former player and assistant manager at the club. His daytime job was to look after the gas lamps in the streets of Uxbridge, but in his spare time he did much to encourage local sport and leisure activities. Next to him, applauding enthusiastically, is well-known Cowley accountant James Sims.

SECTION TEN
OLD TRADES DISAPPEAR

The Uxbridge branch of the Watford-based Sedgwick's Brewery from the north end of the Fassnidge recreation ground, 1960. Brewing ceased at these premises in 1922, and then the Hay-Lambert caramel company moved in.

Fountain's Mill on the River Frays (right), 1960. A flour mill existed here from the fifteenth century and was operated latterly by E. and J. Fountain. Milling ceased in the early 1950s, and the premises were taken over for a while by the Glaxo pharmaceutical company. All of the buildings on the left were demolished in 1969, and the building over the River Frays was altered to become the borough's Adult Training Centre.

The yard of R. Plested's car repair works, Cowley Road, 1969. The firm was established in 1871 as coachmakers and wheelwrights, and here lies a reminder of that bygone era. A completed wheel was bolted securely to this circular base, and a heated iron tyre was slipped over the wheel. Cold water was then poured over the tyre, which immediately contracted and tightened around the wheel.

The premises of Bignell & New electrical contractors, 73 Cowley Road, 1972. Earlier the coal merchant William Muckley was based here, but the use of solid fuel was beginning to decline. In 1950, twelve coal merchants were listed in the *Uxbridge Directory*. By 1970 there were only three. An office block called Frays Court now stands on this site.

Manufacturing plant of the North Thames Gas Board by the canal near Cowley Mill Road, 1965. A gas company was established here in 1854, but production finally ceased in March 1968. Thereafter came the conversion to natural gas, and only the gas holders were required. The buildings were eventually demolished and a newly built Royal Mail sorting office was opened here in 1990.

Jayanbee joinery works by the canal at the western end of Uxbridge High Street, *c*. 1960. A timber yard was established here in 1760 and traded as Osborne Stevens & Co. until 1942. In the aerial view (below) the Fassnidge recreation ground can be seen centre right. The timber business closed in 1966 and the land to the east of the canal was redeveloped as the Highbridge industrial estate. On the western side, formerly Swan and Bottle Meadow, an office block was built for Rank Xerox.

A View of
JAYANBEE'S
EXTENSIVE FACTORY PREMISES
at
UXBRIDGE

Site of the former Lowe & Shawyer cut-flower nurseries, now occupied by Brunel University. Another major change was the closure of this 199-acre nursery, which was established off Kingston Lane in 1868. It ran into difficulties in the post-war period and went into voluntary liquidation in 1958. Above, in October 1962, this flight of greenhouses and a boiler-house were shortly to be cleared away. Below, in March 1965, contractors have moved in to commence building the first phase of the university, seen here from near Station Road, Cowley. The site has been cleared, the southern perimeter road is ready and in the foreground an area for tree planting is being staked out.

Harman's Brewery, 1960s. George Harman founded the business in 1763, and it moved to these premises at 180 High Street in 1875. In 1962 the firm was taken over by Courage, which closed it down two years later. Above; some of the buildings from George Street, with part of the brewery off licence visible on the right. Below: the deserted and forlorn brewery yard seen from the High Street entrance, 1968. Demolition followed two years later, but a gigantic office block erected nearby, called Harman House, keeps the name of the brewery alive.

SECTION ELEVEN
YARDS & ALLEYS

Terraced cottages in Enfield Place, off Villier Street, 1966. These were built as married quarters for the militia, which had a barracks nearby from 1855. The Enfield Close development replaced these humble cottages in 1968.

Yard of the Kings Arms, 1964. The town's first local newspaper was published from outbuildings here in 1860. After the Advertiser moved to larger premises, a rival newspaper called the *Uxbridge Gazette* was published from here. A shortened yard, called Kings Yard, is here today.

Kearley's Yard, between 10 and 11 High Street, 1962. Charles Kearley ran a building business from here in the nineteenth century. One of his sons, Hudson Ewbank Kearley (1856-1934), became the senior partner in Kearley & Tonge wholesale grocers, and was later created Viscount Devonport. At this time the wood-boarded buildings were being used by Percy Constable, a baker. The entrance to the yard has since been filled in.

Beasley's Yard, looking towards the High Street, 1960. This yard, which led to the Old Meeting Church (see p. 82), takes its name from Revd Thomas Ebenezer Beasley, minister of the church from 1790 to 1824. He lived at these premises and also ran a private school for boys here.

The New Inn yard, Windsor Street, May 1967. The inn had then been closed for more than thirty years, and the old stables and outbuildings were in a tumbledown state. Note the splendid metal bath tub at the bottom left. Today the main entrance to Charter Place is here.

Southern end of Chequers Yard, The Lynch, 1968. A car repair firm occupies the former St Margaret's School (right). This yard reached right up to the Chequers Inn in the High Street, but by this time the inn had been demolished. In the distance you can see the twin gables of the George Inn on the opposite side of the road.

Laundry Yard, November 1961. The narrow entrance to this yard was in the High Street opposite the Woolworths store. The laundry with its tall chimney is in the centre and on the right are garages and stores. The building on the left housed the Eldorado Ice Cream Co. in the 1930s, but by this time it was occupied by Chorley Floral Products, a company making artificial plants and flowers.

Laundry Yard in 1960. The laundry building began life as a brewery *c.* 1865, but in 1881 it was altered to become the home of Uxbridge Steam Laundry Co. In the 1920s it was renamed Uxbridge Sanitary Laundry. The business closed in 1962, and the buildings were demolished in October that year.

Laundry Yard from The Lynch end, January 1968. With the old laundry gone, you can see the buildings nearer the High Street. On the left are the side wall of Providence Church and the lime trees in the former graveyard.

Cottages at the Lancaster Road end of Bennett's Yard, late 1960s. The yard takes its name from Michael Bennett, who ran a fish shop by the High Street end in the mid-nineteenth century. These cottages were often called Orchard Place. The external cables indicate that electricity came late to these homes. With tiny rooms and small backyards, it is not surprising that the occupants would often sit outside their front doors in the warm summer evenings. Parts of Bennett's Yard survive today, but the cottages have been replaced by a Child Guidance Centre.

Johnson's Yard, 1967. This yard derives its name from James Johnson, who ran a carrier's business from the yard in early Victorian times, including a daily run to London and back. Above: looking toward the High Street entrance, with the Middlesex Plating Co. on the right. The three-storey house in the distance was built in 1761. Below: looking in the opposite direction. This view changed drastically when Redford Way was opened up in 1969, and Christ Church was built soon afterwards.

Friends' Walk, 1983. This was originally part of the yard of the George Inn, which ran all the way from the High Street to York Road. However, after Bakers Road was opened up, it was renamed because it led to the meeting house of the Society of Friends. That building is just visible in the background, and on the left is the wall of Belmont Road Infants School.

Grainge's Yard, looking from The Lynch, January 1968. The post office building is on the right. Today the yard survives as a service road to the shops on the west side of Windsor Street. It is named after Robert Grainge, who ran an ironmongery business at the High Street end in the mid-nineteenth century. A devout religious man, he was known as 'Bible' Grainge to the townsfolk. A relation, who also ran an ironmonger's shop in the town at the same time, was nicknamed 'Gridiron' Grainge.

Old buildings in Grainge's Yard photographed in January 1968. These lay at the rear of the Howard Roberts grocery shop at 33 High Street, which was a subsidiary of the wholesale grocery firm of Alfred Button & Son Ltd in Belmont Road. A former head of the firm, Sir Howard Button (1873-1943), was a butterfly enthusiast and another of his subsidiary companies called the Vanessa Trading Co. operated from the premises shown here.

More buildings in Grainge's Yard, June 1966. These surely provide us with a glimpse of the tiny cottage homes of the poor. Most of the yards and alleys off the main street were opened up in the early nineteenth century, when rows of small, crowded, insanitary cottages were hastily erected. With no water laid on, primitive latrines and little awareness of hygiene, conditions in these homes were horrific. In 1851 the average age of the people of Uxbridge was twenty-nine.

Janes Place off Vine Street, February 1971. This alley was situated next to the Carpenters Arms (see p. 40) and led to a group of seven cottages built *c.* 1850. From a building on the left hangs the sign of the Uxbridge Car Electrical Co. The Vine Street exit from Charter Place is here today.

Waddington & Son jewellers and watchmakers, 178 High Street, 1969. From about 1840 to 1866, William Atwell ran a similar business from these premises. The yard on the right still bears his name. Atwell's Yard ran from this entrance right up to York Road.

Atwell's Yard, March 1964. An earlier name of this yard was Brewhouse Yard, because it passed through the Harman's Brewery premises. The gas lamp is fixed to the corner of Askew Cottage, which fronted George Street and was so named because it was built in an irregular shape with hardly a right angle to be found.

Top of Atwell's Yard, looking towards York Road, c. 1970. This section of the yard was at one time known as Norton Street and had rows of cottages on either side. The industrial buildings were at one time an iron foundry, and later a timber yard, but by this time they had become part of Robert Lee Ltd, makers of beekeepers' supplies.

Atwell's Yard, 1964. This view of the yard is dominated by the brewery tower and chimney. A small section of the cobbled yard at the High Street end is likely to be preserved, but the part visible here may be converted into a shopping precinct.

SECTION TWELVE
SOME NOTABLE PEOPLE

Alderman George Suter JP, Mayor of Uxbridge 1959-1960. A partner in Suter's Ltd, the family's High Street department store, Suter was a long-serving councillor and president of Uxbridge Cricket Club.

Alderman James Cochrane JP. 'Jimmy' Cochrane was mayor of Uxbridge in 1955, the year in which Uxbridge achieved borough status. He was born at Letham in Scotland, and came to Uxbridge in 1905 to work for the local electricity company. He later set up the Brookside Welding Co. at the western end of Uxbridge High Street. He served on the Urban District Council from 1919 to 1955, and Middlesex County Council from 1942 to 1947. He was made an honorary freeman of the borough in 1956 and died later the same year, aged seventy-two. In 1958 a block of three-storey flats in Vine Street was named Cochrane House in his memory.

Alderman Walter G. Pomeroy JP. Pomeroy was a manager at the local printworks of King & Hutchings. He served on the council from 1932 to 1955 and was its chairman from 1939 to 1946, including the Second World War. At this time he also chaired the Emergency Committee, the Food Control Committee, and the Comforts Fund, which provided gift parcels for members of HM Forces at home and abroad. Pomeroy was the first mayor of Uxbridge borough in 1955/6 and was made an honorary freeman in 1959, shortly after his retirement from public service. He died in 1974, aged eighty-four.

Arthur Kingston FRPS. Kingston was a pioneer of the film industry. He joined the Pathe company in Paris in 1907 and four years later settled in London. In the ensuing period he worked as a newsreel cameraman, but all of the time his inventive powers were coming to the fore. During the First World War he produced improved equipment for aerial photography while serving in the Royal Flying Corps, and after that be devised many modifications and improvements to film equipment. His most significant invention was the plastic lens, which he patented in 1934. Here he is looking at the camera he used to perfect that device. He lived at Old Mill House, Willowbank, and died in 1974, aged eighty-two.

Revd Luther Bouch. Bouch was a native of Aspatria in Cumbria and came to Uxbridge in 1913 to become minister of Old Meeting Congregational Church. He held the pastorate for a remarkable forty-five years. He was a member of the Urban District Council for twenty-eight years and was its chairman from 1934 to 1937. For twenty-five years he served on the local Hospital Board, and he was also on the Rushcliffe Committee, that produced the nurses' charter. He died in April 1960, the day after his seventieth birthday.

Frank and Robert Kirby, 1953. The Kirby brothers are cutting a cake to mark the fortieth anniversary of the founding of their ironmongery shop in Uxbridge High Street. From this small beginning Kirby Bros Ltd became the largest firm of builders' merchants for miles around, employing more than 250 people. In the mid-1950s they had four shops in the High Street and warehouses in Warwick Place. 'Mr Frank' (left) died in 1955 and 'Mr Bob' in 1966. In 1971 the name Kirby disappeared following a takeover of the company.

Management team of E.E. Chaney & Sons Ltd, corn merchants, outside their Lawn Road premises on the occasion of the firm's centenary, 1965. Left to right: Don Chaney (managing director), Tom Dell (accounts), Kitty Treagus (secretary), E.R.D. 'Tim' Chaney (chairman) and Robert Dell (accounts assistant). The town centre redevelopment forced Chaney's to move to Hubbards Farm at Hillingdon in 1968. Since 1983 there has been no Chaney family connection with Chaney Ltd.

Bob (left) and Bill Buckledee in their Vine Street electrical, radio and TV store, 1960. Radio-controlled vans were being introduced to give a swifter and more efficient service to customers, and the necessary equipment is visible behind the brothers. The firm of Buckledee & Tayler was founded at 50 Vine Street in 1924 by their father, John Robert Buckledee, and his partner, Arthur Tayler. The redevelopment of Vine Street led to the closure of the firm in 1977.

Mrs Kate Fassnidge in the garden of her house, The Cedars, 66 High Street. Kate Canham was engaged to Sidney Fassnidge, a solicitor, for years. His mother opposed the match, so the couple waited until she died. They eventually married in 1917, when Sidney was fifty-nine and Kate was fifty-four. Alas, Sidney died four years later. Kate died in 1950, leaving a request that a horsedrawn hearse, not a motor vehicle, should convey her to her last resting place. This was done. She left The Cedars and its lovely garden to Uxbridge Council, expressing the wish that her house should become 'a public library or rest centre to be designated the Fassnidge Memorial Hall', and that her garden should become an extension to the Fassnidge recreation ground. These wishes have not been carried out (see p. 116). The Fassnidge family originated in Buckinghamshire and have been traced back to the twelfth century in the area around Hughenden and Great Missenden. Daniel and Benjamin Fassnidge came to Uxbridge *c.* 1780, and the building firm of Fassnidge & Son was established *c.* 1796. A merger in 1934 led to the firm being renamed Fassnidge Son & Norris Ltd. It moved from Uxbridge in 1990.

SECTION THIRTEEN
MORE CHANGES IN SOCIETY

The majestic perambulator. This fine vehicle gradually disappeared in the period covered by this book. It was replaced by the folding 'buggy', which fitted into the boot of a car.

The garden at The Cedars, left to the town council by Mrs Kate Fassnidge in 1961 (see p. 114). This haven of tranquility was not to last. In 1969 most of the garden was taken for the Cedars roundabout, part of the town's relief road system.

Outing of members of Uxbridge Old People's Welfare Association, June 1958. Mrs Fassnidge's house was found to be unsuitable for the use she intended, and no satisfactory use has yet been found. A building called Fassnidge Hall was erected in the garden and became the home of Uxbridge Old People's Welfare Association, which was founded in 1956. These members are on a coach outing to Wannock Gardens, Polegate.

Policeman on point duty at the junction of the High Street and Windsor Street, *c.* 1950. The market house and St Margaret's church are in the background. For nearly twelve hours a day, in all weathers, an officer was on duty here directing the traffic. Early in 1954, traffic-lights were installed at this junction – the first in the district.

BSA A7 and sidecar, 1972. The increase in car ownership also led to the gradual disappearance of the motor-cycle combination. At this time there were very few examples of this model left. Gone were the delights of wearing heavy clothes and goggles, and facing wind and weather.

At the Court at Buckingham Palace

The 17th day of March, 1955

Present:

THE QUEEN'S MOST EXCELLENT MAJESTY
IN COUNCIL

WHEREAS there was this day read at the Board a Report of a Committee of the Lords of Her Majesty's Most Honourable Privy Council, dated the 15th day of March, 1955, in the words following, viz.:—

"The Lords of the Committee, in pursuance of the Local Government Act, 1933, having taken into consideration a humble Petition of the Council of the Urban District of Uxbridge, in the Administrative County of Middlesex, praying for the grant of a Charter creating the said Urban District a Municipal Borough and incorporating the inhabitants thereof, do this day agree humbly to report, as their opinion, to Your Majesty, that a Charter may be granted by Your Majesty in terms of the Draft hereunto annexed."

Her Majesty, having taken into consideration the said Report, and the Draft Charter accompanying it, was pleased, by and with the advice of Her Privy Council, to approve thereof, and to order, as it is hereby ordered, that the Right Honourable Gwilym Lloyd-George, one of Her Majesty's Principal Secretaries of State, do cause a Warrant to be prepared for Her Majesty's Royal Signature, for passing under the Great Seal a Charter in conformity with the said Draft, which is hereunto annexed.

W. G. Agnew.

Notice of approval of a charter to create the urban district of Uxbridge a municipal borough. It was in the 1930s that the idea first arose that the Uxbridge Urban District Council should apply for borough status. Apart from the township, the area covered included Cowley, Hillingdon, Ickenham and Harefield. The Second World War delayed the process, but in the post-war years the campaign was renewed. Success came in 1955, and the Charter of Incorporation was handed over by HRH the Duchess of Kent at a ceremony in the Regal cinema.

Coat of arms of the Borough of Uxbridge. The new borough was granted its coat of arms and crest. It can be described using non-heraldic terms as follows: on the shield the triangular shape was part of the arms of the former urban district; the eagle was taken from the arms of the Earl of Uxbridge and was also a reminder of the presence of RAF Uxbridge and RAF Northolt; the circles containing wavy lines represent the waterways of the district; the crest above the shield shows the English lion, holding a Saxon sword from the arms of Middlesex; the chrysanthemums, said to be unique in civic heraldry, represent the horticultural nurseries in the borough.

Borough of Uxbridge

Presentation of the

FREEDOM OF ENTRY INTO THE BOROUGH

TO

THE ROYAL AIR FORCE UXBRIDGE

AT

Royal Air Force Station Uxbridge

on Saturday, 19th March, 1960

at 2.30 p.m.

G. A. SUTER, J.P.
Mayor

E. RONALD WEST
Town Clerk

Cover of programme from the presentation to the RAF station of the freedom of entry into the borough. In 1960 the borough granted freedom of entry to the RAF station at Uxbridge. A ceremony on the main parade ground was followed by a march through the town led by the Central Band. On that day the RAF station was granted 'the privilege and honour, henceforth and for ever, of marching through the streets of the Borough of Uxbridge on all ceremonial occasions with drums beating, colours flying, swords drawn and bayonets fixed'. The annual parade continues to this day.

Part of the procession passing the Eight Bells public house, 19 March 1960. This was a day on which the citizens of the borough expressed their appreciation of the achievements of RAF Uxbridge. The Royal Flying Corps, as it was then known, took over the Hillingdon House Estate in 1917 which became the Armament and Gunnery School for the remainder of the First World War. In 1918 the RFC became the RAF, and in 1920 the Central Band was transferred to the Uxbridge camp. In the post-war years RAF Uxbridge also became the acceptance centre where new recruits were issued with their uniforms and did their initial 'square-bashing'. An underground operations room played a major role in winning the Battle of Britain, because all of the fighter squadrons in south-east England were controlled from there. The Queen's Colour Squadron, the crack drill unit, is now based at Uxbridge.

The last meeting of the Council of the Borough of Uxbridge, March 1965. On this occasion the mayor, aldermen and councillors were joined by some of the principal officers. Although years of effort and preparation had gone into the formation of the borough, it was destined to last only ten years. Reorganization of local government in the entire Greater London area led to the creation of the London Borough of Hillingdon in April 1965. The Borough of Uxbridge then merged with three adjoining urban districts: Hayes and Harlington, Yiewsley and West Drayton, and Ruislip and Northwood. Front row, left to right: Alderman A.H. Streets, Alderman L. Davies, Alderman C.J. Gadsden, Alderman T. Parker, Councillor D. Samuel (deputy mayor), Councillor Mrs W. Pomeroy (mayor), E. Ronald West (town clerk), Alderman S.L. Meggeson, Alderman Mrs L. Wane, Alderman G. Hartley and Alderman N. Holland. Councillors on the middle row: K. Marlow, L. Sherman, Miss Amor Wilkins, F. Sutcliffe, B. Simpson, K. Drury, E. Ing, A. Wye, E. Wood, Mrs B. Thorndike and R.H. Nicholls-Pratt. Back row: W. Duncan, T.L. Morgan, G. Preston, T Wright, J. Coleman, J, Wells, P Flower, J. Ball, T. Barnard, W. Winton, P. Kidby and R. Bossom. Council officers on the left: P.L. Osborne (deputy engineer), L.C. Alexander (deputy town clerk), A.W Caudery (housing), C.S. Manning (deputy treasurer), E.B. Pearson (treasurer), O.C. Dobson (medical officer of health), A.J. Benson (chief clerk of public health) and H.E.G. Stripp (engineer/surveyor). Right: S.H. Stansfield (solicitor), A.A.L. Playfair (administrative and committee clerk), H.H. Willis (parks), W.M. Drake (town clerk's department), J. Brass (mace bearer), W.C.H. Harris (committee clerk), D.A. Jones (committee clerk) and R. Smith (committee clerk).

The Mayor and Deputy Mayor wore red robes, while those of the Councillors were black. Aldermen's robes were trimmed with fur, and the ladies are shown wearing black tricorn hats. Formal dress doubtless gave an air of dignity and earnestness to council meetings.

In the last month of its existence, Uxbridge Council found that it had a surplus of about £400,000 in its housing fund. Approval was therefore hastily given to a number of building projects in what the local press inevitably called 'a spending spree'. The schemes adopted were the building of flats and maisonettes in Nursery Waye, flats at Cornfield Close, and two tower blocks of flats in Chiltern View Road. The third of these developments was later modified, and only one thirteen-storey block was built. It was named Rabbs Mill House, and was officially opened in June 1967.

Greengrocer's market barrow, New Inn yard, May 1967. This barrow was being used by a stallholder in the nearby market house, but a closer inspection revealed that it had originally been in use at Brentford Market. This barrow and the bath tub behind seemed even then to belong to a bygone age.

Territorial Army armoured car, Elthorne Road, February 1966. It is lunchtime on a Sunday and the men of the Territorial Army have nipped into the Militia Canteen in Elthorne Road for a quick pint, leaving their tank unattended outside! There was clearly no threat of terrorism at that time. In Queen Victoria's reign a detachment of the Royal Elthorne Light Infantry Militia had been stationed in barracks nearby, thus giving the pub its name.

Demolition of the main buildings of the Uxbridge Union Workhouse, December 1967. This former parish workhouse was established on this site in 1747, and it was from this that Hillingdon Hospital developed following a 1929 Act of Parliament. The transformation began in the 1930s and continued apace in the post-war years. The Duchess of Kent maternity wing opened in 1960 and a ten-storey block of wards followed in 1967.

Breakspear Crematorium, Ruislip, 1970. This building, set in twenty acres of woodland, opened in January 1958. At this time many people still found cremation unacceptable, often for religious reasons. By 1964, however, one Uxbridge undertaker was reporting a noticeable swing in favour and that 60 per cent of his business was then concerned with cremation. Increased acceptance followed and the West Chapel was added in 1973.

The day after the fire at the King & Hutchings printworks, 24 January 1968. A huge pall of black smoke rose over Uxbridge when part of the printing works in Cricketfield Road caught fire. Nearly a hundred firemen with twenty appliances fought the blaze – the biggest in Uxbridge for many years. Tons of newsprint, ink and chemicals went up in smoke. This area was later totally cleared, and an office block called Boundary House now stands on the site.

Aftermath of the King & Hutchings fire, looking from the site of Vine Street station. Visible here are the charred remains of large rolls of newsprint. Plant and equipment worth about £750,000 were destroyed, and it was several days before firemen were certain that the fire was completely out. Although a major setback at the time, the blaze gave the printing company the opportunity to introduce new technology into their printing processes in a purpose-built building nearby.

Engineering department under construction at Brunel College, early 1966. Brunel College of Advanced Technology had outgrown its site at Acton and was about to move to the Uxbridge campus (see p. 95). In June 1966 the college was granted its charter, and it was therefore at Brunel University that the first students arrived on the Kingston Lane site in the autumn of 1967.

Work proceeding on a new shopping precinct, looking from Belmont Road, August 1969. High-rise blocks of offices were also being built. On the right are the Uxbridge branch of Barclays Bank and the White Horse public house. The first of the new shops opened in December 1970, but the precinct was a bleak and dreary place. Nevertheless, the shrewd positioning of the post office, and the arrival in Uxbridge of Marks & Spencer and Tesco, ensured its commercial viability. In the 1980s the Prudential Corporation took over the site, put a glass roof over the shopping area and relaunched the improved precinct as The Pavilions.

Index